BUSINESS ISSUES, COMPETITION AND ENTREPRENEURSHIP

AF680847

# GOVERNMENT CONTRACTS AND SMALL MINORITY-OWNED BUSINESSES

## CHALLENGES AND ASSISTANCE

# BUSINESS ISSUES, COMPETITION AND ENTREPRENEURSHIP

Additional books in this series can be found on Nova's website under the Series tab.

Additional E-books in this series can be found on Nova's website under the E-book tab.

BUSINESS ISSUES, COMPETITION AND ENTREPRENEURSHIP

# GOVERNMENT CONTRACTS AND SMALL MINORITY-OWNED BUSINESSES

## CHALLENGES AND ASSISTANCE

GREGOR MEIJIR
EDITOR

NOVINKA

New York

Copyright © 2013 by Nova Science Publishers, Inc.

**All rights reserved.** No part of this book may be reproduced, stored in a retrieval system or transmitted in any form or by any means: electronic, electrostatic, magnetic, tape, mechanical photocopying, recording or otherwise without the written permission of the Publisher.

For permission to use material from this book please contact us:
Telephone 631-231-7269; Fax 631-231-8175
Web Site: http://www.novapublishers.com

**NOTICE TO THE READER**

The Publisher has taken reasonable care in the preparation of this book, but makes no expressed or implied warranty of any kind and assumes no responsibility for any errors or omissions. No liability is assumed for incidental or consequential damages in connection with or arising out of information contained in this book. The Publisher shall not be liable for any special, consequential, or exemplary damages resulting, in whole or in part, from the readers' use of, or reliance upon, this material. Any parts of this book based on government reports are so indicated and copyright is claimed for those parts to the extent applicable to compilations of such works.

Independent verification should be sought for any data, advice or recommendations contained in this book. In addition, no responsibility is assumed by the publisher for any injury and/or damage to persons or property arising from any methods, products, instructions, ideas or otherwise contained in this publication.

This publication is designed to provide accurate and authoritative information with regard to the subject matter covered herein. It is sold with the clear understanding that the Publisher is not engaged in rendering legal or any other professional services. If legal or any other expert assistance is required, the services of a competent person should be sought. FROM A DECLARATION OF PARTICIPANTS JOINTLY ADOPTED BY A COMMITTEE OF THE AMERICAN BAR ASSOCIATION AND A COMMITTEE OF PUBLISHERS.

Additional color graphics may be available in the e-book version of this book.

**Library of Congress Cataloging-in-Publication Data**

ISBN: 978-1-62618-713-9

*Published by Nova Science Publishers, Inc. † New York*

# CONTENTS

# PREFACE

Each year, the government obligates billions in contracts to businesses, nearly $537 billion in fiscal year 2011. About $104 billion (19.4 percent) was obligated to small businesses that identified themselves as minority-owned. In this book, the Government Accountability Office (GAO) describes what federal agency officials and advocacy groups identified as challenges small, minority-owned businesses may face in seeking federal government contracts, including and linguistic or cultural barriers, and agencies efforts to address them; and what information is available on federal efforts to assist small, minority-owned businesses in contracting with the federal government.

Chapter 1 - Each year, the government obligates billions in contracts to businesses— nearly $537 billion in fiscal year 2011. About $104 billion (19.4 percent) was obligated to small businesses, and over $36 billion of this amount was obligated to small businesses that identified themselves as minority-owned (see figure). In this report, GAO describes (1) what federal agency officials and advocacy groups identified as challenges small, minority-owned businesses may face in seeking federal government contracts— including any linguistic or cultural barriers—and agencies' efforts to address them, and (2) what information is available on federal efforts to assist small, minority-owned businesses in contracting with the federal government. For selected agencies, GAO analyzed data on obligations to minority-owned businesses, reviewed information on programs and resources that can assist minority-owned businesses, reviewed relevant information from the Department of Justice on agencies' Limited English Proficiency plans, and interviewed officials from selected federal agencies and advocacy groups that provide assistance to minority-owned businesses. In written comments, Commerce said that GAO had not covered all federal efforts to support small, minority-owned business contracting. As GAO noted in the report, this study focused on selected agencies and contracting activities that accounted for about 70 percent of total federal obligations to small, minority-owned businesses in fiscal year 2010.

Chapter 2 - Commonly known as the "8(a) Program," the Minority Small Business and Capital Ownership Development Program is one of several federal contracting programs for small businesses. The 8(a) Program provides participating small businesses with training, technical assistance, and contracting opportunities in the form of set-asides and sole-source awards. A "set-aside" is an acquisition in which only certain contractors may compete, while a sole-source award is a contract awarded, or proposed for award, without competition. In FY2011, the federal government spent $16.7 billion on contracts and subcontracts with 8(a) firms. Other programs provide similar assistance to other types of small businesses (e.g., women-owned, HUBZone).

Eligibility for the 8(a) Program is generally limited to small businesses "unconditionally owned and controlled by one or more socially and economically disadvantaged individuals who are of good character and citizens of the United States" that demonstrate "potential for success." Each of these terms is further defined by the Small Business Act, regulations promulgated by the Small Business Administration (SBA), and judicial and administrative decisions.

A "business" is generally a for-profit entity that has a place of business located in the United States and operates primarily within the United States or makes a significant contribution to the U.S. economy by paying taxes or using American products, materials, or labor. A business is "small" if it is independently owned and operated; is not dominant in its field of operations; and meets any definitions or standards established by the Administrator of Small Business. Ownership is "unconditional" when it is not subject to any conditions precedent or subsequent, executory agreements, or similar limitations. "Control" is not the same as ownership and includes both strategic policy setting and day-to-day administration of business operations.

Members of certain racial and ethnic groups are presumed to be socially disadvantaged, although individuals who do not belong to these groups may prove they are also socially disadvantaged. To be economically disadvantaged, an individual must have a net worth of less than $250,000 (excluding ownership in the 8(a) firm and equity in one's primary residence) at the time of entry into the 8(a) Program. This amount increases to $750,000 for continuing eligibility. In determining whether an applicant has good character, SBA looks for criminal conduct, violations of SBA regulations, or current debarment or suspension from federal contracting. For a firm to have demonstrated "potential for success," it generally must have been in business in the field of its primary industry classification for at least two years immediately prior to applying to the 8(a) Program. However, small businesses owned by Indian tribes, Alaska Native Corporations (ANCs), Native Hawaiian Organizations (NHOs), and Community Development Corporations (CDCs) are eligible for the 8(a) Program under somewhat different terms.

The 8(a) Program has periodically been challenged on the grounds that the presumption that members of certain racial and ethnic groups are disadvantaged violates the constitutional guarantee of equal protection. The outcomes in early challenges to the program varied, with some courts finding that plaintiffs lacked standing because they were not economically disadvantaged. Most recently, a federal district court found that the program is not unconstitutional on its face because "breaking down barriers to minority business development created by discrimination" constituted a compelling government interest, and the government had a strong basis in evidence for concluding that race-based action was necessary to further this interest. However, the court found that the program was unconstitutional as applied in the military simulation and training industry because there was no evidence of public- or private-sector discrimination in this industry.

In: Government Contracts …
Editor: Gregor Meijir

ISBN: 978-1-62618-713-9
© 2013 Nova Science Publishers, Inc.

*Chapter 1*

# GOVERNMENT CONTRACTING: FEDERAL EFFORTS TO ASSIST SMALL MINORITY-OWNED BUSINESSES*

*United States Government Accountability Office*

## ABBREVIATIONS

| | |
|---|---|
| CCR | Central Contractor Registration |
| CMR | Commercial Market Representative |
| DHS | Department of Homeland Security |
| DOD | Department of Defense |
| DOJ | Department of Justice |
| FAR | Federal Acquisition Regulation |
| FPC | Federal Procurement Center |
| FPDS-NG | Federal Procurement Data System-Next Generation |
| GSA | General Services Administration |
| HHS | Department of Health and Human Services |
| HUBZone | Historically Underutilized Business Zone |
| LEP | Limited English Proficiency |
| MBDA | Minority Business Development Agency |

* This is an edited, reformatted and augmented version of The United States Government Accountability Office publication, Report to Congressional Requesters GAO-12-873, dated September 2012.

| | |
|---|---|
| OSDBU | Office of Small and Disadvantaged Business Utilization |
| PCR | Procurement Center Representative |
| PTAC | Procurement Technical Assistance Center |
| PTAP | Procurement Technical Assistance Program |
| SAM | System for Award Management |
| SBA | Small Business Administration |

## WHY GAO DID THIS STUDY

Each year, the government obligates billions in contracts to businesses—nearly $537 billion in fiscal year 2011. About $104 billion (19.4 percent) was obligated to small businesses, and over $36 billion of this amount was obligated to small businesses that identified themselves as minority-owned (see figure). In this report, GAO describes (1) what federal agency officials and advocacy groups identified as challenges small, minority-owned businesses may face in seeking federal government contracts— including any linguistic or cultural barriers—and agencies' efforts to address them, and (2) what information is available on federal efforts to assist small, minority-owned businesses in contracting with the federal government. For selected agencies, GAO analyzed data on obligations to minority-owned businesses, reviewed information on programs and resources that can assist minority-owned businesses, reviewed relevant information from the Department of Justice on agencies' Limited English Proficiency plans, and interviewed officials from selected federal agencies and advocacy groups that provide assistance to minority-owned businesses. In written comments, Commerce said that GAO had not covered all federal efforts to support small, minority-owned business contracting. As GAO noted in the report, this study focused on selected agencies and contracting activities that accounted for about 70 percent of total federal obligations to small, minority-owned businesses in fiscal year 2010.

## WHAT GAO FOUND

While their views varied to some degree, federal agency officials and advocacy groups GAO contacted identified a number of challenges that small, minority-owned businesses may face in pursuing federal government contracts. For example, officials and advocacy groups pointed to a lack of performance history and knowledge of the federal contracting process as significant barriers. Officials from advocacy groups cited additional challenges, such as difficulty gaining access to contracting officials and decreased contracting opportunities resulting from contract bundling—the consolidation of two or more contracts previously performed under smaller contracts, into a single contract. Officials from agencies that accounted for 70 percent of federal contracting with small, minority-owned businesses—(the Departments of Defense, Health and Human Services, and Homeland Security, and the General Services Administration) told GAO that they conducted outreach to help small, minority-owned businesses with these challenges. Their outreach efforts include one-on-one interviews between contracting office staff and businesses seeking federal contracts. Linguistic and cultural barriers were identified as a challenge on a limited basis.

**Percentage of Obligated Funds for Contracts to Small, Minority-Owned Businesses, Fiscal Year 2011**

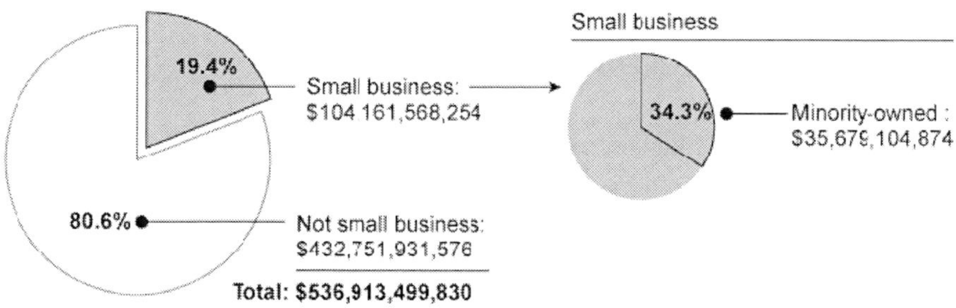


Source: GAO analysis of data from Federal Procurement Data System – Next Generation.

Federal agencies GAO contacted collected and reported some information on the contracting assistance provided to small disadvantaged businesses—including those that are minority-owned. Two agencies GAO reviewed collected and reported data by minority group. The Minority Business Development Agency in the Department of Commerce—created to foster the growth of minority-owned businesses of all sizes—reported that its business centers helped these businesses obtain 1,108 financings and contracts worth over $3.9 billion in fiscal year 2011. For the same fiscal year, the Small Business Administration (SBA) reported that more than 90 percent of its primary business development program participants were minority-owned businesses. Federal agencies that GAO contacted said that the goals SBA negotiated with federal agencies for contracting with various socioeconomic categories, including small disadvantaged businesses, provided some information on efforts to assist minority-owned businesses. In fiscal year 2011, agencies GAO contacted met their prime contracting goal and three out of four agencies met their subcontracting goals. GAO generally found limited data on participants in agency outreach efforts because the agencies are not required to, and therefore generally do not, collect data on the minority group or socioeconomic category of businesses that participate in outreach events for federal contracting opportunities.

September 28, 2012

The Honorable Elijah Cummings
Ranking Member
Committee on Oversight and Government Reform
House of Representatives

The Honorable Judy Chu
House of Representatives

The Honorable Mike Honda
House of Representatives

The Honorable Gary Peters
House of Representatives

The federal government has a long-standing policy of maximizing procurement opportunities for small businesses owned and controlled by socially and economically disadvantaged individuals (small disadvantaged businesses).[1] In 1978, Congress amended the Small Business Act to require federal agencies to, among other things, negotiate annually in good faith with the Small Business Administration (SBA) to establish prime and subcontracting goals for these businesses, which include businesses owned and controlled by various minority groups.[2]

U.S. Census data show that minority-owned businesses are among the fastest growing businesses in the U.S.[3] According to the 2007 Survey of Business Owners—the most recent survey data available—minorityowned businesses numbered 5.8 million, an increase of 45.5 percent over the 5 years prior to the survey and more than double the 17.9 percent rate for all U.S. businesses over the same time period.

Federal contracting can be an important revenue source for businesses of any size. In fiscal year 2011, federal agencies obligated a total of around $537 billion in government contracts to businesses. [4] About $104 billion was obligated to small businesses (19 percent) and of this amount, just over one-third ($36 billion) was obligated to small businesses that identified themselves as minority-owned according to data from the Federal Procurement Data System-Next Generation (FPDS-NG).[5] To foster participation by small disadvantaged and minority-owned small businesses in federal contracting, federal agencies administer a number of programs and conduct outreach activities for them. For example, SBA administers programs that are designed to develop small businesses— including minority-owned businesses—and help them navigate the federal contracting process. Federal agencies also participate in outreach activities such as matchmaking events—one-on-one meetings—that bring together agency contracting officials and businesses seeking contracts. Further, all federal agencies with procurement authority are required by law to have an Office of Small and Disadvantaged Business Utilization (OSDBU) that works specifically on contracting issues for these businesses.[6] Finally, a number of online resources are available to all businesses seeking federal contracting opportunities.

Given the growth in minority-owned business, you asked us to assess procurement programs that assist minority-owned businesses. For this report, we reviewed (1) what federal agency officials and advocacy groups identified as challenges that small, minority-owned businesses seeking federal government contracts may face—including linguistic or cultural barriers—and agencies' efforts to address them, and (2) what information is available on the extent of federal efforts to assist small, minority-owned businesses in contracting with the federal government.

To determine what federal agency officials and advocacy groups identified as challenges that minority-owned businesses may face in contracting with the federal government, we interviewed agency officials from a purposive, non-representative sample of eight contracting offices at four agencies that accounted for about 70 percent of total federal obligations to small, minority-owned businesses in fiscal year 2010.[7] The officials included those from contracting offices (those responsible for making acquisition decisions) and OSDBUs. The four agencies were the Departments of Defense (DOD), Health and Human Services (HHS), and Homeland Security (DHS), and the General Services Administration (GSA). We also interviewed officials from SBA and the Minority Business Development Agency (MBDA), a part of the Department of Commerce that was set up specifically to assist minority-owned businesses of all sizes. In addition, we interviewed officials from advocacy groups that provide assistance to businesses owned by Asian-, Black-, Hispanic-, and Native-Americans.

To describe the information available on the extent of federal agencies' efforts to assist small, minority-owned businesses in contracting with the federal government, we reviewed federal government prime contracting and subcontracting goals, SBA procurement scorecards, and documentation describing programs that can provide contracting assistance to minority-owned businesses. We conducted interviews with officials from the selected agencies and their contracting offices to identify and obtain information available on their outreach efforts to contract with minority-owned businesses. In addition, we conducted interviews with 12 advocacy groups that provided contracting assistance to the minority groups in our scope. Appendix I provides additional details about our objectives, scope, and methodology.

We conducted this performance audit from November 2011 through September 2012 in accordance with generally accepted government auditing standards. Those standards require that we plan and perform the audit to obtain sufficient, appropriate evidence to provide a reasonable basis for our findings and conclusions based on our audit objectives. We believe that the evidence obtained provides a reasonable basis for our findings and conclusions based on our audit objectives.

# BACKGROUND

## Federal Goals for Contracting with Small Businesses

Under the Small Business Act, SBA plays an important role in ensuring that small businesses gain access to federal contracting opportunities. SBA negotiates specific agency-wide goals to ensure that the federal government collectively meets the 23 percent statutory goal for contract dollars awarded to small businesses.[8] In addition, SBA negotiates goals for the socioeconomic categories of businesses. The current goals are:

- 5 percent of prime contracts and subcontract dollars are to be awarded to women-owned small businesses,

- 5 percent of prime contracts and subcontract dollars are to be awarded to small disadvantaged businesses,
- 3 percent of prime contracts and subcontract dollars are to be awarded to service-disabled veteran-owned small businesses, and
- 3 percent of prime and subcontract dollars are to be awarded to HUBZone small businesses.

Appendix II provides more information on the extent that federal agencies obligated federal contract dollars to minority-owned businesses by various socioeconomic categories.

## Federal Agency Contracting Assistance for Small Businesses

The federal government has established a number of programs that can assist small and small disadvantaged businesses—including those that may be minority-owned—that seek to contract with federal agencies. MBDA promotes the growth and competitiveness of minority-owned businesses of any size.[9] MBDA's network of business centers helps clients identify federal procurement opportunities, analyze solicitations, and prepare bids and proposals. It also facilitates relationships between minority-owned businesses and federal agencies, and researches contracting trends at federal agencies. MBDA's Federal Procurement Center (FPC) provides research on federal agency contracting trends, identifies large federal contracts, and helps minority-owned businesses identify possible contracting opportunities.

SBA administers programs that are targeted to small businesses and that provide assistance with federal contracting opportunities. SBA's 8(a) Business Development Program is one of the federal government's primary means of developing small businesses owned by socially and economically disadvantaged individuals. [10] Participating businesses, which are generally referred to as 8(a) firms, are eligible to participate in the program for 9 years. Businesses receive technical assistance, mentoring, counseling, and financial assistance so that they can become competitive in the federal marketplace. Additionally, participating businesses may bid on competitive federal contracts that are open only to 8(a) firms as well as on noncompetitive federal contracts.[11]

SBA's Procurement Center Representatives (PCR) and Commercial Market Representatives (CMR) play an important role in helping ensure that small businesses gain access to contracting and subcontracting opportunities.[12] PCRs and CMRs are the primary SBA staff who implement SBA's prime contracts and subcontracting assistance programs, which are intended to increase contracting opportunities for small businesses and help ensure that small businesses receive a fair and equitable opportunity to participate in federal prime contracts and subcontracts. PCRs also can make recommendations to agency contracting officers that proposed contracts be set aside for eligible small businesses.[13] In particular, a PCR's key responsibilities include reviewing potentially bundled or consolidated solicitations—those in which two or more procurement requirements previously provided or performed under separate smaller contracts are grouped into a solicitation for a single contract[14]—and making set-aside recommendations to agency contracting officers.

The OSDBU within federal agencies advocate on behalf of small businesses. Section 15(k) of the Small Business Act describes the functions of OSDBU directors—which include implementing and executing the agency's functions and duties related to the award of contracts and subcontracts to small and small disadvantaged businesses.[15] Other responsibilities of the OSDBU include identifying bundled contracts, potentially revising them to encourage small business participation, and facilitating small business participation in the contracts. OSDBU directors also help small businesses obtain payments from agencies and subcontractors, recommend set-asides, coordinate with SBA, and oversee OSDBU personnel.[16]

Agencies also conduct outreach activities for small and small disadvantaged businesses, including minority-owned firms that are seeking federal contracts. Some agencies host monthly vendor outreach sessions, a series of appointments with either agency officials (such as small business or procurement officials) or prime contractors that have subcontracting needs. These sessions give the businesses an opportunity to discuss their capabilities and learn about potential contracting opportunities. One of MBDA's primary outreach efforts is the Minority Enterprise Development Week Conference. During this conference, participants from minority-owned businesses that have been vetted and designated by MBDA are offered appointments with federal and corporate partners to discuss contracting opportunities that will be made available within the next 6 to 18 months.

Finally, a number of online resources are also available to businesses seeking to contract with the federal government. For example, federal agencies list their contract solicitations of $25,000 or more on the Federal Business Opportunities website (www.FedBizOpps.gov)–managed by GSA. The website provides online business tools, training videos, and event announcements for small business owners. USA Spending, established by the

Office of Management and Budget, also contains information on federal spending trends across the government, including grants and contracts. In addition, federal agencies such as SBA provide online contracting courses designed to help small businesses understand the basics of contracting with government agencies.[17] Appendix III provides a summary of selected programs, resources, and outreach activities available to minority-owned businesses.

# AGENCIES AND ADVOCACY GROUPS IDENTIFIED VARIOUS CONTRACTING CHALLENGES THAT MINORITY-OWNED BUSINESSES MAY FACE

Agency and advocacy group officials we interviewed identified a number of challenges that small businesses—including minority-owned businesses—may face when seeking to contract with the federal government. In particular, these officials generally agreed that the lack of performance history and knowledge of the federal contracting process were significant challenges minority-owned businesses may face in contracting with the federal government. However, the officials offered varying opinions on the extent to which minority-owned businesses faced other challenges, such as a lack of access to contracting officials and a lack of monitoring subcontracting plans, and difficulties accessing needed resources such as capital. Some agency officials we contacted indicated that outreach activities they conduct and practices they undertake in their contract solicitation activities address some of these challenges.

## Agency and Advocacy Group Officials Differed in Their Opinions on Contracting Challenges That Minority-Owned Businesses May Face

### *Performance History*

Federal agency and advocacy group officials that we interviewed differed in their opinions on challenges that small businesses—including those that are minority-owned—may face when seeking to contract with the federal government. The challenges identified included a lack of performance history and knowledge of the federal contracting process, contract bundling, a lack of access to contracting officials, lack of monitoring of subcontracting plans, and difficulties assessing capital.

Officials from federal agencies and advocacy groups we contacted cited the lack of a performance history and a full understanding of the federal contracting process as significant challenges that minority-owned businesses may face. According to the statement of Guiding Principles of the Federal Acquisition System, when selecting contactors to provide products or perform services, the government will use contractors that have a track record of successful past performance or that have demonstrated a current superior ability to perform.[18] SBA officials told us that historically and currently, small, minority-owned businesses that lacked a performance history have had difficulty entering the federal contracting market. MBDA officials also said that lack of a past performance record with government contracts or private contracts of similar size, made obtaining federal contracts more difficult for minority-owned businesses because of the weight given to performance history.[19]

However, some agency officials, including those from two DHS contracting offices, noted that because prior commercial experience—not just government contracting experience—was considered, the lack of prior government experience would not necessarily make a minority-owned business noncompetitive. Officials from a GSA contracting office said that most small businesses seeking to contract with its office had a performance history with the private sector, not the federal government. The officials said that they considered past performance with the private sector when making contract award decisions, and thus would not consider lack of past performance history with the federal government as a challenge. Finally, officials from an HHS contracting office noted that the Federal Acquisition Regulation (FAR) requires that businesses receive a neutral rating if they do not have a performance history and that some small businesses may not be aware of this requirement.[20] However, some advocacy group officials indicated that certain prerequisites and past performance requirements were difficult for minority-owned businesses to meet. For example, officials from one group said that these businesses might partner with other more established businesses to help meet the performance requirements.

### *Knowledge of the Federal Contracting Process*

Some federal agency and advocacy group officials we contacted indicated that lack of knowledge of the federal contracting process can be a challenge for businesses seeking these contracts. For example, one advocacy group official noted that small businesses have to understand the work of the agencies, such as if there are any prerequisites, certifications, or specialized skill sets that are required to obtain contracts. In addition, an OSDBU official from DHS said that minority-owned businesses could experience challenges in obtaining information about various contracting opportunities, learning and understanding how the bidding process works, and learning how to secure a government contract. Further, MBDA officials noted that the federal contracting process was very different from contracting with private sector companies. They added that although federal agencies spend time and money holding sessions on doing business with the federal government, these sessions offered general information that could not be transferred to bidding on specific projects. Similarly, agency officials also cited the lack of understanding of agencies' contracting needs. For example, an OSDBU official from HHS emphasized that businesses that did not understand the mission of the agency with which they were seeking a contract or did not know what the agency bought and acquired might not know how to market their product or service appropriately to win the contract.

### *Contract Bundling*

Advocacy group officials cited contract bundling as a significant challenge, although a majority of agency officials disagreed. Advocacy group officials whom we interviewed said that contract bundling could reduce the number of contracting opportunities available for small and minority-owned businesses. MBDA officials said that they believe that many contracts are bundled unnecessarily and agreed that this practice limited minority-owned businesses' ability to compete for these contracts.

However, other federal agency officials we interviewed said that they did not believe that contract bundling was a significant challenge for minority-owned businesses at their agencies. In addition, some agency officials told us that they had specific policies regarding contract bundling. For example, HHS and DOD contracting officials noted that their offices had policies that prohibited contract bundling and added that small businesses could protest a contract that they believed was unjustifiably bundled.[21] Further, officials from one HHS contracting office indicated that they worked with small business specialists to determine if contracts should be separated.

### *Lack of Access to Contracting Officials*

Advocacy group officials cited a lack of access to contracting officials as a significant challenge. Officials from six advocacy groups that we interviewed stated that the agency officials present at outreach events, such as matchmaking events, often did not have the authority to make decisions about awarding a contract. However, with the exception of MBDA, none of the federal agency officials we contacted said that access to contracting officers was a challenge at their agencies. The officials emphasized efforts that their agencies were making to assist businesses. For example, officials participate in industry days, where businesses can meet prime contractors as well as interact with agency procurement staff, and also conduct one-on-one appointments with businesses that seek to contract with their agencies. Some federal contracting officials did note that limited resources might pose a challenge in accessing the contracting officers. For example, contracting officials from DHS and GSA indicated that any perceived access issues would be due to limited resources in contracting offices. GSA contracting officials said that when the office had a large number of contracts to complete, they could not meet with each business owner seeking contract opportunities.

***Lack of Monitoring of Subcontracting Plans***

Advocacy group officials also cited a lack of monitoring of subcontracting plans by federal agencies as a significant challenge for minority-owned businesses, although SBA officials noted that this issue was a challenge for all small businesses, not just those owned by minorities. Officials from five advocacy groups described instances in which prime contractors did not use the small, minority-owned business subcontractors that they initially said they would use. Further, one advocacy group official said that because federal contracting officials generally had relationships with prime contractors and not subcontractors, small, minority-owned subcontractors often had no recourse when a problem arose. An official from another advocacy group stated that contracting officers have no accountability to federal agencies to justify any subcontractor changes. SBA officials noted that prime contractors' "dropping" of subcontractors from their plans after the contracts were obligated was not an issue exclusive to minority-owned businesses but was a challenge for small subcontractors in general.[22]

In addition, we previously reported that CMRs cited a lack of authority to influence subcontracting opportunities.[23] PCRs and CMRs also said that it was difficult to enforce prime contractors' performance under subcontracting plans because determining that a contractor was not acting in good faith was difficult. Officials from one DOD contracting office said that they did not communicate with subcontractors directly and that prime contractors did have the right to pick a subcontractor of their choice throughout the duration of a contract. An OSDBU official from DOD added that the contracting officer would review and approve a replacement subcontractor under certain circumstances. If a prime contractor's subcontracting plan included a certain percentage of work that was designated for a small disadvantaged business, the contracting officer might not approve the proposed replacement subcontractor if the change did not adhere to the original percentage.

### *Lack of Access to Capital and Other Resources*

Some federal agency and advocacy group officials we interviewed said that a lack of access to capital, financing, and bonding were challenges. Officials from three federal agencies, including contracting officials and one OSDBU official, cited lack of access to capital as a key barrier for minority-owned businesses. SBA officials also said that historically and currently small, minority-owned businesses have had difficulty entering the federal contracting market due to lack of access to capital. In addition, according to a 2010 MBDA report, capital access is the most important factor limiting the establishment, expansion, and growth of minority-owned businesses. Moreover, MBDA reported that minority-owned businesses paid higher interest rates on loans than other businesses, received smaller loans, were more likely to be denied credit, and were less likely to apply for loans because they feared their applications would be denied.[24]

Further, officials from two advocacy groups noted that bonding requirements could prevent small, minority-owned businesses from competing for large contracts. Bonding is required to compete for certain contracts to ensure that businesses have the financial capacity to perform the work and pay for labor and supplies.[25] For example, an official at one advocacy group indicated that to be considered for large contracts, businesses may be required to obtain $25 million to $50 million in bonding capacity. Since few small businesses can obtain this bonding capacity, this official said that these businesses rely on "teaming" arrangements—two or more businesses that collectively pursue larger procurement contracts—to expand their opportunities.

### *Linguistic and Cultural Barriers*

In general, advocacy groups identified linguistic and cultural barriers as a challenge for minority-owned businesses on a limited basis. One advocacy group official said that linguistic barriers may be a challenge because business owners with strong accents could have difficulty communicating. Officials from a few Asian-American advocacy groups noted that business owners with limited English proficiency (LEP) [26] may experience challenges. For example, one official said that business owners in the construction industry may have difficulty obtaining a required design certification if English was not the business owner's first language. Another advocacy group official cited challenges such as discrimination against subcontractors by prime contractors because of accents or LEP. Officials from advocacy groups also cited examples of cultural barriers. For example, one noted that some first generation Americans might have an aversion to working with the federal government and therefore would not be willing to seek government contracts. Some officials from Hispanic advocacy groups said Hispanic contracting officials were underrepresented in the federal government.

Officials from another group also said that some minority groups, including those in nonmetropolitan areas, could lack the infrastructure needed (e.g., Internet service and transportation) to conduct business in these areas.

Officials from all but one federal agency—SBA—that we contacted said that they did not know of any linguistic or cultural issues that posed a barrier for minority-owned businesses seeking to contract with the government. SBA officials told us that cultural barriers may be a challenge for minority-owned businesses seeking federal government contracts and emphasized that minority-owned businesses would be hesitant to reveal any linguistic barriers. The officials noted that some cultural barriers existed for Asian-Americans, Alaskan Natives, Native-Americans, and Native Hawaiians, because their traditional ways of conducting business involved intangibles that did not translate well into a "faceless" electronic contracting community. These officials also said that some minority-owned businesses may have informal business practices—for example, they may obtain financing from a friend or family member instead of through a bank—and therefore a business owner might not have the documentation required by some federal programs.

## Agency Outreach Efforts Help Address Some Challenges Facing Small and Minority-Owned Businesses

As we have previously noted, federal agencies conduct outreach to help minority-owned businesses seeking federal government contracts. For example, federal contracting officials with whom we spoke cited "industry days," conferences, and meetings with businesses as efforts to help businesses address challenges they could face in seeking federal contracts. During industry days small businesses are invited to meet prime contractors in their industries and potentially obtain subcontracts. Businesses can also interact directly with contracting office staff. For example, contracting officers said that they participated in panel discussions to provide business owners with information on the acquisition process and forecasts of contract opportunities. Contracting officers also accept requests from business owners that schedule meetings to discuss their business capabilities. Many agency officials, including an OSDBU official and contracting officials, told us they also work with and refer businesses to Procurement Technical Assistance Centers (PTAC) so that the businesses may receive one-on-one assistance.

Agency outreach to businesses is generally directed by agency OSDBUs, the agencies' advocates for small businesses. OSDBU directors use a variety of methods—including internal and external collaboration, outreach to small businesses, and oversight of agency small business contracting—to help small businesses overcome challenges they may face such as understanding the federal contracting process. OSDBU officials from three federal agencies we contacted indicated that they collaborate with several agency offices, such as acquisition and small business specialists, and with organizations such as MBDA. We previously reported that nearly all of the OSDBU directors saw outreach activities as a function of their office.[27] For example, 23 of the 25 OSDBU directors we surveyed between November and December 2010 viewed hosting conferences for small businesses as one of their responsibilities, and 23 had hosted such conferences. More specifically, these 23 agencies had hosted an average of 20 conferences within the previous 2 years. In addition, 20 of the 25 OSDBU directors surveyed saw sponsoring training programs for small businesses as one of their responsibilities, and 18 had hosted such events in the last 2 years.

## Federal Agencies Collect Some Information on Contracting Assistance Provided to Minority-Owned Businesses

Federal agencies we contacted generally collect and report information on contracting assistance they provide to small and small disadvantaged businesses. Federal agencies are required to report annually to SBA on participation in the agency's contracting activities by small disadvantaged businesses, veteran-owned small businesses (including service-disabled veterans), qualified HUBZone small businesses, and women-owned small businesses. SBA compiles and analyzes the information and reports the results to the President and Congress.[28] Agencies are also required to report to SBA plans to achieve their contracting goals, which can include outreach activities. In addition, Executive Order 11,625 requires the Secretary of Commerce—the umbrella agency of MBDA—and other agencies to report annually on activities related to minority business development and to provide other information as requested. Finally, federal agencies are also required to develop and implement systematic data collection processes and provide MBDA with current data that will help in evaluating and promoting minority business development efforts.[29]

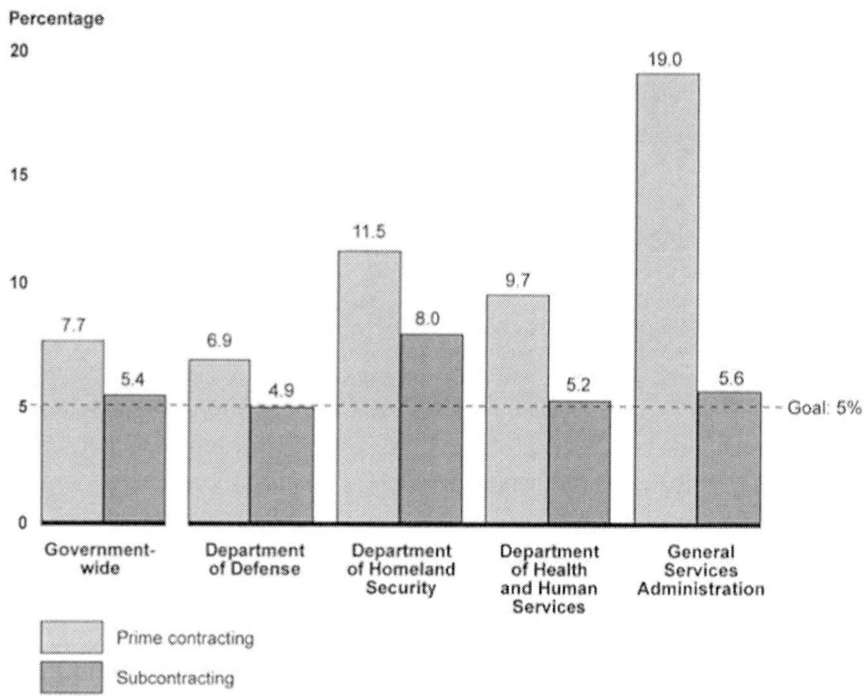


Source: SBA data.

Figure 1. Government-wide and Selected Agency Prime and Subcontracting Goal Achievement, Small Disadvantaged Businesses, Fiscal Year 2011.

A majority of the federal agencies we contacted told us that the extent to which they met SBA prime and subcontracting goals for the various socioeconomic categories of businesses (including the small disadvantaged business goal) provided a measure of their efforts to assist minority-owned businesses in contracting with the federal government. As figure 1 shows, in fiscal year 2011 the federal government met its 5 percent goal for prime contracting and subcontracting with small disadvantaged businesses. In addition, all four agencies we reviewed met their prime contracting goals of 5 percent, and three met their 5 percent subcontracting goals for this category. Contracting officials at these agencies generally attributed their success in contracting with small businesses—including small disadvantaged businesses—to a variety of factors, including support from the agency OSDBU and upper management, staff commitment, and the use of set-asides. They also noted several other factors that contributed to their contracting performance, including market research, a strategy for small businesses, and outreach efforts.

Federal agency officials also said that some outreach activities might be targeted to certain socioeconomic categories to assist in meeting agency SBA goals.

For example, DHS contracting office officials said that as a result of monitoring their progress in meeting SBA goals, they conducted outreach to women-owned and HUBZone businesses with contract set-asides.

SBA also issues an annual scorecard as an assessment tool to measure how well federal agencies reach their small business and socioeconomic prime contracting and subcontracting goals, to provide accurate and transparent contracting data, and to report agency-specific progress. An overall grade assesses an agency's entire small business procurement performance, and three quantitative measures show achievements in prime contracting, subcontracting, and plan progress, or an agency's efforts and practices to meet its contracting goals.[30] An overall grade is given for government-wide performance, and individual agencies receive their own grades. For fiscal year 2011, SBA gave a grade of "B" for overall government-wide performance. For the federal agencies that we included in our analysis, GSA scored an overall grade of A+, DHS and HHS scored an overall grade of A, and DOD scored an overall grade of B. Two agencies we reviewed collected and reported data by minority group.

For example, MBDA reports data categorized by minority group, on contracting assistance that its business centers provide as required by executive order.

For fiscal year 2011, MBDA reported that its business centers helped minority-owned businesses obtain 1,108 transactions (the sum of contracts and financings) totaling over $3.9 billion (see table 1).[31]

**Table 1. MBDA Client Assistance by Minority Group, Fiscal Year 2011**

| Minority groups | Number of contracts | Number of financings | Total transactions | Dollar value of contracts | Dollar value of financings | Total dollar value of awards |
|---|---|---|---|---|---|---|
| African American | 217 | 102 | 319 | $1,264,362,499 | $826,639,729 | $2,091,002,228 |
| Asian American | 23 | 28 | 51 | 114,456,719 | 24,444,285 | 138,901,004 |
| Asian Indian | 16 | 18 | 34 | 58,707,052 | 19,956,625 | 78,663,677 |
| Asian Pacific American | 27 | 10 | 37 | 12,817,685 | 16,606,632 | 29,424,317 |
| Hasidic Jew | 63 | 3 | 66 | 17,025,583 | 74,210,000 | 91,235,583 |
| Hispanic American | 155 | 76 | 231 | 539,874,743 | 438,981,088 | 978,855,831 |
| Native American | 217 | 51 | 268 | 126,392,998 | 409,191,757 | 535,584,755 |
| Other minority | 59 | 43 | 102 | 980,134 | 12,569,948 | 13,550,082 |
| Total | 777 | 331 | 1,108 | $2,134,617,413 | $1,822,600,064 | $3,957,217,477 |

Source: MBDA.

SBA also collects some information for its various programs, including information by minority group for the 8(a) Business Development Program, as required by statute.[32] For example, SBA reported that of the 7,814 8(a) program participants in fiscal year 2011—the most recent data available—more than 90 percent of the participants were minority-owned businesses (see fig. 2). SBA also reported that 8(a) program participants reported total year-end revenues exceeding $21.7 billion in fiscal year 2010, with 43.4 percent of these revenues coming from 8(a) contracts. During that same year, SBA provided technical assistance to 2,000 8(a) businesses. SBA officials we interviewed said that SBA generally did not collect information by minority group for any of its other programs.

Most federal agencies that we contacted indicated that they collected some general information on outreach events and activities and some demographic data, although collecting such data was not required. For example, for outreach events such as the Minority Enterprise Development week conference, MBDA officials told us that they collect general demographic information from participants on their businesses and experience, but not by minority group. The officials told us that they also collect aggregated data on its outreach activities for minority-owned businesses, such as number of meetings and participants.

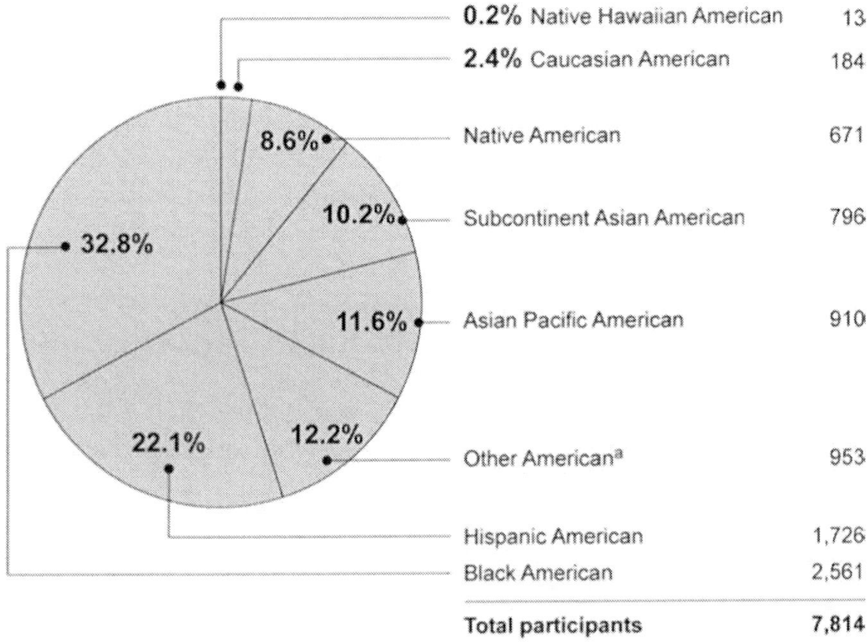


Source: SBA.

[a] According to SBA, the category of "other American" includes individuals who select this category, who select "no ethnicity", who select categories that are not considered an ethnicity or race, and who make no selection at all. In SBA's fiscal year 2011 survey of 8(a) participants, "other American" included 221 Alaskan Native corporations, 80 tribally owned organizations, 17 Native Hawaiian organizations, and 2 community development organizations.

Figure 2. 8(a) Program Participants, by Minority Group, Fiscal Year 2011.

For example, MBDA officials told us that they conducted 119 of the 129 one-on-one meetings scheduled between minority-owned and small businesses and corporations and prime contractors during this event.

Officials from DOD, DHS, GSA, and HHS said that they asked participants in their outreach events questions (sometimes by survey or evaluation) about the value or helpfulness of the events. Officials from three agencies noted that they used the survey results to determine the effectiveness of, or how to improve, the event. In addition, agencies may ask questions to obtain general information about a business and potentially its socioeconomic status. Officials also said that they collected some information by socioeconomic group, but none by minority group.

Finally, the OSDBU Council—which comprises OSDBU officials from various federal agencies—hosts an annual procurement conference that provides assistance to businesses seeking federal government contracts, and some information is collected for this event.[33] According to the council's website, more than 3,500 people registered for the 2012 conference, and more than 130 matchmaking sessions were conducted. According to the council's president, 2012 is the first year that such information was collected.

## AGENCY COMMENTS AND OUR EVALUATION

We provided a draft of this report to Commerce, DHS, DOD, GSA, HHS, and SBA for review and comment and received comments only from Commerce.

Commerce made two observations on our draft report. First, the department stated that the report was a good start at capturing the federal government's effort to support small, minority-owned businesses, but did not include all federal programs that supported federal contracting with minority-owned businesses. The department added that GAO had missed an opportunity to provide a more comprehensive picture of the federal government's efforts in this area, noting, for example, that the Departments of Agriculture, Housing and Urban Development, and Transportation had programs (other than OSDBUs) geared toward increasing federal contracts with minority-owned firms. In addition, the department stated that an Office of Minority and Women Inclusion was recently established at each of the financial regulatory agencies. While providing support to minority-owned businesses, these agencies and offices were outside of the scope of our review, which as we stated in our report, focused on the four agencies—DHS, DOD, GSA, and HHS—that accounted for about 70 percent of total federal obligations to small, minority-owned businesses in fiscal year 2010. We also included SBA and Commerce's MBDA in our review because of their roles in assisting minority-owned businesses. We are reviewing the efforts of the Office of Minority and Women Inclusion in an ongoing study that will be issued in 2013.

Second, Commerce noted that although the dollar amount of federal contracts obligated to small, minority-owned businesses was encouraging, the report did not analyze the number of minority-owned firms that actually secured federal contracts. The department said that it was possible that a handful of minority-owned firms had secured sizable federal contracts but that the majority of minority-owned firms continued to fail in obtaining them.

However, data are not available on the total universe of small, minority-owned businesses that entered bids in response to federal contract solicitations. Just as with our reporting of funds obligated for contracts, data on the number of minority-owned businesses that secured federal contracts would not provide information on the number of such businesses that did not obtain them. Likewise, while we do report MBDA's statistics on contracting assistance provided to minority-owned businesses, again such data do not provide information on how many businesses sought but did not obtain federal contracts. We conducted interviews with officials from MBDA, SBA, contracting offices at the federal agencies in our scope, and advocacy groups to obtain their perspectives on the challenges minority-owned businesses may face in seeking to contract with the federal government.

William B. Shear
Director,
Financial Markets and Community Investment

## Appendix I: Objectives, Scope, and Methodology

Our objectives were to describe: (1) what federal agency officials and advocacy groups identified as challenges that small, minority-owned businesses may face in seeking to contract with the federal government—including any linguistic or cultural barriers—and agencies' efforts to address them, and (2) what information is available on federal efforts to assist small, minority-owned businesses in contracting with the federal government.

To determine which programs and resources to include in our scope, we conducted a web-based search for initial information on programs and resources available from federal government agencies using terms such as contracting assistance for minorities. We analyzed information on programs that provide federal contracting assistance and resources on contracting opportunities, and are available to minority-owned businesses. We describe programs and resources provided by the Minority Business Development Agency (MBDA) as they are tasked with the growth and promotion of minority-owned businesses. We also describe programs and resources available from the Small Business Administration (SBA), as this agency is responsible for providing assistance to small businesses—which can be minority owned—and programs and resources available from other selected federal agencies based on the criteria described below.[1] Finally, we interviewed officials from these selected agencies and advocacy groups that provide assistance to businesses owned by Asian-, Black-, Hispanic-, and Native-Americans. We selected these minority groups because they received the largest share of federal obligations to small, minority-owned businesses based on business owners self-identifying as a member of these groups.

To select agencies to include in our scope, we reviewed data from Federal Procurement Data System-Next Generation (FPDS-NG) on contract awards to small businesses owned by the minority groups in our scope by federal agency. Although we could not independently verify the reliability of these data, we reviewed system documentation and conducted electronic data testing for obvious errors in accuracy and completeness. On the basis of these efforts, we determined that the FPDS-NG data on federal contract dollars to socioeconomic groups by self-reported minority group were sufficiently reliable for purposes of our review. We selected the top four agencies that accounted for about 70 percent of total federal obligations to small, minority-owned businesses in fiscal year 2010—the most recent data available at the time of our selections. These agencies were the Departments of Defense (DOD), Health and Human Services (HHS), and Homeland Security (DHS), and, the General Services Administration (GSA).

To select a purposive, non-representative sample of contracting offices for purposes of conducting interviews, we first selected the top two divisions within DOD, DHS, and HHS in terms of the percentage of their agency's obligations to small, minority-owned businesses.[2] Those divisions included the Departments of the Army and Navy for DOD; the Bureau of Customs and Border Protection and the United States Coast Guard for DHS, and the National Institute of Health and the Centers for Medicaid and Medicare for HHS. We selected only one division for GSA—the Public Buildings Service—as this division represented over 76 percent of GSA's funds obligated for contracts to small, minority-owned businesses. Using this approach, we selected a total of seven divisions within the four agencies in our scope. Within each division, we selected one of the top contracting offices based on the office's percentage of their division's obligations to businesses owned by the minority groups in our scope. We selected two contracting offices from the Department of the Army because the percentage of obligations to small, minority-owned businesses by any of its top contracting offices was small. Our final sample consisted of eight contracting offices.

To describe the challenges that small, minority-owned businesses may face in contracting with the federal government, we interviewed agency officials—including those from contracting offices and the Office of Small

Disadvantaged Business Utilization—from the purposive, nonrepresentative sample of eight contracting offices. We also interviewed officials from MBDA and SBA. Further, we conducted interviews with officials from 12 advocacy groups. We selected groups that provided assistance to businesses owned by the minority groups in our scope based on a web-based search on national organizations that represent and provide assistance to minority-owned businesses in obtaining federal contracts. To describe information on improving access to services for persons with limited English proficiency, we reviewed Executive Order 13,166—*Improving Access to Services for Persons with Limited English Proficiency* (LEP)—to understand its applicability to outreach activities associated with federal contracting. We reviewed guidance from the Department of Justice (DOJ), as well as existing LEP plans for each agency in our scope. We could not review the LEP plans for DOD and for SBA, as the plan for each agency had not yet been completed. We also obtained and reviewed written responses from DOJ.

To describe the information available on the extent of federal efforts to assist small, minority-owned businesses in contracting with the federal government, we reviewed federal government prime contracting and subcontracting goals and SBA procurement scorecards for fiscal year 2011 for DOD, HHS, DHS and GSA. We also reviewed documentation for programs that assist small businesses owned and controlled by socially and economically disadvantaged individuals—which can include businesses that are minority-owned—to determine the types of contracting assistance available. We conducted interviews with officials from the selected agencies and contracting offices to identify and obtain available information on their outreach efforts to assist minority-owned businesses. In addition, we conducted interviews with officials from 12 advocacy groups that provide contracting assistance to the minority groups in our scope.

For information on the percentage of funds obligated for contracts in fiscal year 2011 to each socioeconomic category of small businesses by minority group—including small disadvantaged, women-owned, service-disabled veteran-owned, and Historically Underutilized Business Zone (HUBZone)—we analyzed data from FPDS-NG, which receives data from the Central Contractor Registration System (CCR)—the system in which all businesses seeking federal government contracts must register. In CCR, registrants (i.e., business owners) can self identify as minority-owned and can specify a minority group(s). Registrants can select from the following six categories: Asian Pacific, Subcontinent Asian, Black-American, Hispanic-American, Native-American, and Other. We conducted electronic testing for obvious errors in accuracy and completeness. As a part of this assessment, we analyzed the FPDS-NG data to determine cases in which contracting firms were identified as belonging to a particular minority group, such as Subcontinent Asian, but did not designate the firm as being minority-owned. This occurred in less than 3 percent of the cases. We conducted the same assessment within different socioeconomic categories, such as small disadvantaged business, and found a potential undercount of the minority-owned designation in less than 4 percent of the cases.

In addition, businesses that selected "other minority" and those that self-identified as more than one minority group were categorized as other minority. We determined the minority-owned designations data were sufficiently reliable for the purposes of our report. However, because we cannot verify the minority group that contractors self-report, we characterize these data as self-reported.

We conducted this performance audit from November 2011 through September 2012 in accordance with generally accepted government auditing standards.

Those standards require that we plan and perform the audit to obtain sufficient, appropriate evidence to provide a reasonable basis for our findings and conclusions based on our audit objectives. We believe that the evidence obtained provides a reasonable basis for our findings and conclusions based on our audit objectives.

# Appendix II: Percentage of Obligated Funds for Contracts to Socioeconomic Categories by Minority Group, Fiscal Year 2011

We analyzed data from the Federal Procurement Data System – Next Generation to determine the amount of obligated funds for contracts that federal agencies made to small businesses by minority group for fiscal year 2011. As figure 3 shows, the federal government obligated over $36 billion (35.1 percent) to small, minority-owned businesses in fiscal year 2011. Figure 4 shows the amount of federal obligated funds for contracts to small disadvantaged businesses. For example, about $28.8 billion (85.6 percent) was obligated to small disadvantaged businesses that were minority-owned. Figures 5 shows the amount of federal obligated funds for contracts to small women-owned businesses. For example, $8.2 billion (45.7) percent were obligated to small women-owned businesses that were minority-owned.

Figure 6 shows the amount of federal obligated funds for contracts to small HUBZone businesses. For example, nearly $5.5 billion (54.3 percent) were obligated to small HUBZone businessсs that were minority- owned.

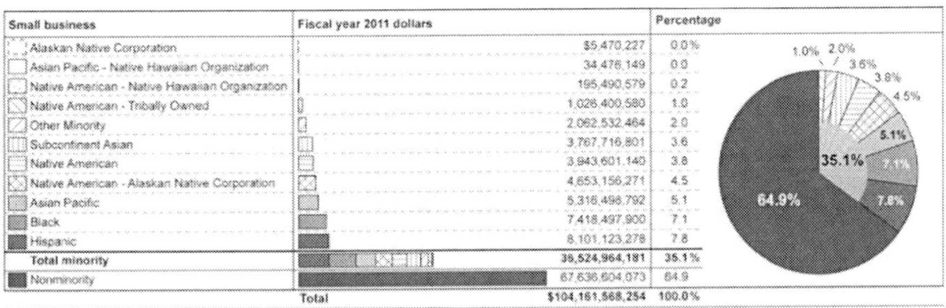


Source: GAO Analysis of Federal Procurement Data System – Nest Generation.

Note: Data are as of February 2012. The dollars reported are in obligations and minority designations are self-reported. Businesses that self identified as "other minority" and those that selected more than one minority category were designated as other minority. Nonminority includes those that did not select any minority category.

Figure 3. Percentage of Obligated Funds for Contracts to Small Businesses by Minority Group, Fiscal Year 2011.

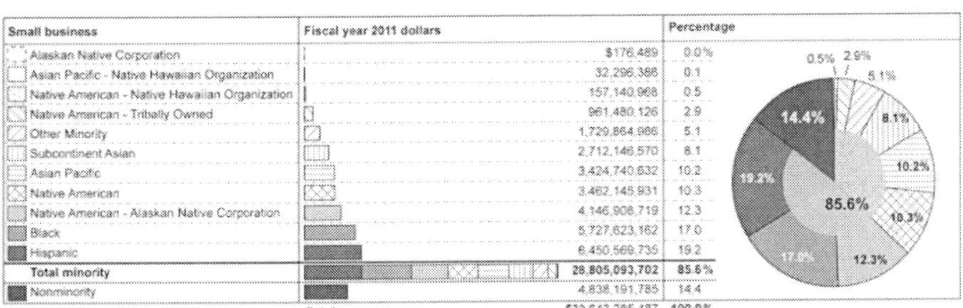


Source: GAO Analysis of Federal Procurement Data System – Nest Generation.

Note: Data are as of February 2012. The dollars reported are in obligations and minority designations are self-reported. Businesses that self identified as "other minority" and those that selected more than one minority category were designated as other minority. Nonminority includes those that did not select any minority category.

Figure 4. Percentage of Obligated Funds for Contracts to Small Disadvantaged Businesses by Minority Group, Fiscal Year 2011.

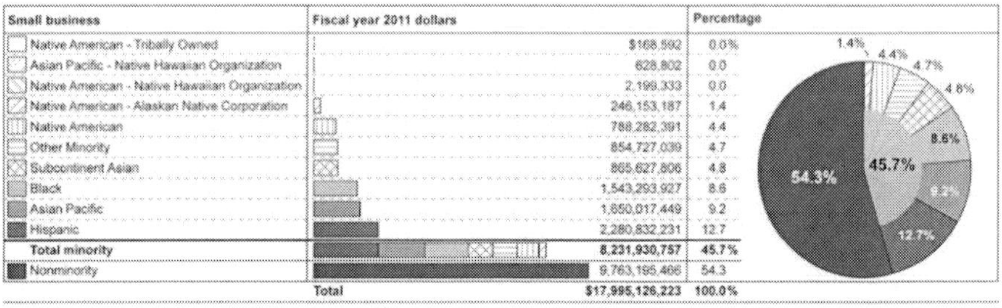


Source: GAO Analysis of Federal Procurement Data System – Nest Generation.

Note: Data are as of February 2012. The dollars reported are in obligations and minority designations are self-reported. Businesses that self identified as “other minority” and those that selected more than one minority category were designated as other minority. Nonminority includes those that did not select any minority category.

Figure 5. Percentage of Obligated Funds for Contracts to Small Women-Owned Businesses by Minority Group, Fiscal Year 2011.

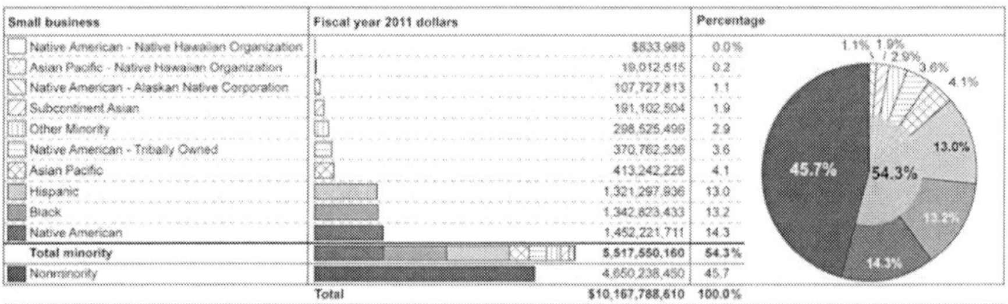


Source: GAO Analysis of Federal Procurement Data System – Nest Generation.

Note: Data are as of February 2012. The dollars reported are in obligations and minority designations are self-reported. Businesses that self identified as “other minority” and those that selected more than one minority category were designated as other minority. Nonminority includes those that did not select any minority category.

Figure 6. Percentage of Obligated Funds for Contracts to Small HUBZone Businesses by Minority Group, Fiscal Year 2011.

Figure 7 shows the amount of federal obligated funds for contracts to small service-disabled veteran-owned businesses. For example, nearly $3.9 billion (33 percent) were obligated to small service-disabled veteran-owned businesses that were minority-owned.

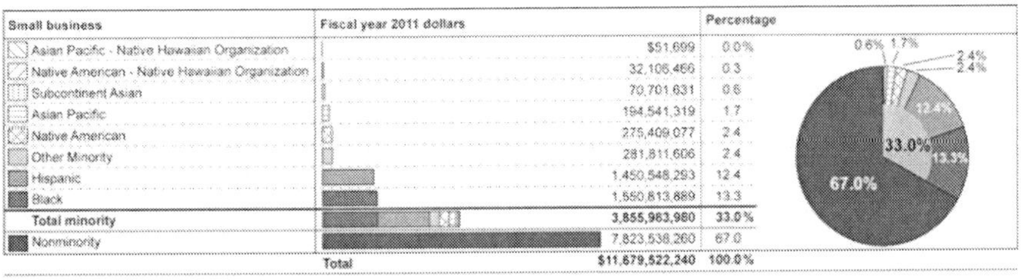


Source: GAO Analysis of Federal Procurement Data System – Nest Generation.

Note: Data are as of February 2012. The dollars reported are in obligations and minority designations are self-reported. Businesses that self identified as "other minority" and those that selected more than one minority category were designated as other minority. Nonminority includes those that did not select any minority category.

Figure 7. Percentage of Obligated Funds for Contracts to Small Service-Disabled Veteran-Owned Businesses by Minority Group, Fiscal Year 2011.

# Appendix III: Selected Federal Government Contracting Programs, Resources, and Outreach Activities

This table shows programs, resources, outreach activities, and examples of contracting assistance that agencies provide to assist minority-owned businesses in contracting with the federal government.

**Table 2. Selected Federal Programs, Resources and Outreach Activities**

| Program or resource (agency) | Description | Examples of contracting assistance provided |
|---|---|---|
| Programs | | |
| Business Centers (MBDA) | MBDA funds a nationwide network of business centers which operate as public/private partnerships that provide direct client assistance and educate businesses on how to do business with the federal government and private sector. | •Identification of procurement opportunities based on client needs and sourcing deals<br>•Solicitation analysis<br>•Bid and proposal preparation<br>•Research contract award |

**Table 2. (Continued)**

| Program or resource (agency) | Description | Examples of contracting assistance provided |
|---|---|---|
| Programs | | |
| | | histories<br>•Post-award contract administration<br>•Central contractor registration<br>•Certification assistance |
| Federal Procurement Center (FPC) (MBDA) | Supported by MBDA's new Governmental Procurement Unit, the FPC is the first business center in the U.S. that assists minority-owned businesses in competing for and winning federal government contracts. | •Identification of federal procurement opportunities<br>•Facilitation of relationships between minority-owned businesses and federal program managers<br>•Research on federal agency contracting trends<br>•Information on federal regulations and contracting requirements<br>•Linking minority-owned businesses with other companiesto develop strategic partnerships |
| 8(a) Business Development Program (SBA) | The 8(a) program is a 9-year developmental program that provides technical and management assistance to businesses so that they can become competitive in the federal marketplace. | •8(a) businesses may be eligible for set-asides, awards exclusively for program participants |
| Procurement Assistance to Small Businesses Program | This program assists small businesses in obtaining a fair share of contracts and subcontracts for federal government supplies and services and a fair share of property sold by the government. | •Application of small business set-asides to increase procurement to small businesses<br>•Consultation with procuring activities on structuring of procurement and sales planning to optimize small business participation |

| Program or resource (agency) | Description | Examples of contracting assistance provided |
|---|---|---|
| Programs | | |
| | | •Review and analysis of small businesses' capacity<br>•Review of subcontracting plans and programs of large prime contractors to determine the extent that they are providing subcontracting opportunities to the SBA socioeconomic categories. |
| Procurement Technical Assistance Cooperative Agreement Program (PTAP) (DOD) | PTAP was created to generate employment and to improve the general economy of a locality by assisting business firms in obtaining and performing under federal, state, and local government contracts. | PTAP established Procurement Technical Assistance Centers (PTAC) that assist small businesses seeking to contract with DOD and with other agencies by providing the following:<br><br>•counseling,<br>•matchmaking, and<br>•assistance with online database registration |
| Mentor-Protégé Program (Various) | The mentor-protégé program includes an arrangement in which mentors—typically businesses that are experienced prime contractors—provide technical, managerial, and other business development assistance to eligible small businesses. | Mentor-protégé agreements authorize a broad array of developmental assistance such as<br><br>•assistance in obtaining certifications needed to work on large federal government contracts<br>•contract administration<br>•loans and award of subcontracts on a noncompetitive basis[a] |
| *Other Resources* | | |
| Office of Small and Disadvantaged Business Utilization (Various) | OSDBUs are advocates for contracting opportunities for small and disadvantaged businesses. | OSDBUs functions include<br><br>•identifying proposed |

**Table 2. (Continued)**

| Program or resource (agency) | Description | Examples of contracting assistance provided |
|---|---|---|
| Programs | | |
| | | solicitations that involve significant bundling of contract requirements<br>•working with agency procurement officials to revise such proposed solicitations to increase the probability of participation by a small business<br>•advising agency leadership on small business matters<br>•providing direction for developing and implementing policies and initiatives to help ensure that small businesses have the opportunity to compete for and receive a fair share of agency procurements |
| Procurement Center Representatives (SBA) | PCRs help ensure that small businesses gain access to contracting opportunities. | PCR's key responsibilities include<br><br>•reviewing proposed agency solicitations—such as potentially bundled and consolidated solicitations<br>•making set-aside recommendations to agency contracting officers<br>•reviewing agency small business programs |

| Program or resource (agency) | Description | Examples of contracting assistance provided |
|---|---|---|
| Programs | | |
| | | •counseling small businesses[b] |
| Commercial Market Representatives (CMR) (SBA) | CMRs help ensure that small businesses gain access to subcontracting opportunities. | CMRs' key responsibilities include<br><br>•counseling small businesses on marketing themselves toprime contractors<br>•counseling large prime contractors on maximizing subcontracting opportunities for small businesses<br>•facilitating the matching of prime contractors with small businesses |
| Minority Enterprise Development (MED) Week Conference (MBDA) | MED Week Conference, one of MBDA's primary outreach efforts, offers thousands of minority-owned businesses across a variety of industries the opportunity to connect with buyers, and access information, tools, and resources to grow their businesses. | During MED Week, businesses are provided the following assistance<br><br>•15-minute appointments with federal and corporate partners to discuss upcoming contracting opportunities<br>•educational sessions on topics such as capital access<br>•discussions about federal contracting opportunities with representatives from agencies' Offices of Small and Disadvantaged Business Utilization (OSDBU) |

**Table 2. (Continued)**

| Program or resource (agency) | Description | Examples of contracting assistance provided |
|---|---|---|
| Programs | | |
| Federal Business Opportunities (www.FedBizOpps.gov) | FedBizOpps is the single point of entry for federal buyers to publish and for businesses to find federal business opportunities over $25,000 across departments and agencies. | Businesses can conduct ad hoc searches or set up automaticqueries to notify them when opportunities meeting their criteria are posted |
| BusinessUSA (www.businessusa.gov) | BusinessUSA is a centralized, one-stop platform for businesses to access services to help them grow and hire. | The site allows small businesses and exporters to use technology to quickly connect to the services and information relevant to them, regardless of where the information is located or which agency's website, call center, or office they go to for help |
| USA Spending (www.usaspending.gov) | USAspending.gov is a free, publicly accessible website containing data on federal awards (e.g., contracts, loans, grants) across the government. | For each award, the site includes<br><br>•the name of the entity receiving the award<br>•the amount of the award<br>•information on the award such as transaction type and funding agency<br>•the location of the entity receiving the award<br>•a unique identifier of the entity receiving the award |
| Federal Procurement Data System- Next Generation (FPDS-NG) | FPDS-NG is a comprehensive web-based tool and database that functions as a clearinghouse for all federal contract actions exceeding $3,000. | FPDS-NG allows businesses to obtain information on how federal contract funds are being spent government-wide |
| *Outreach activities* | | |
| Matchmaking Events (Various) | Matchmaking events are held around the country to give business owners the opportunity to meet prime | During matchmaking events businesses are provided the following |

| Program or resource (agency) | Description | Examples of contracting assistance provided |
|---|---|---|
| Programs | | |
| | contractors and agency contracting officers. | assistance<br><br>•insights into doing business with agencies<br>•cultivating effective relationships with prime contractors |
| Vendor Outreach Sessions | Monthly sessions consisting of 10-to 15-minute appointments with either agency officials (such as small business or procurement officials) or prime contractors that have subcontracting needs. The sessions may be geared to SBA socioeconomic categories. | Vendor outreach sessions include<br><br>•discussions on business' capabilities<br>•information on potential contracting opportunities<br>•meetings with individuals who have decision-making responsibilities |

Source: GAO analysis of agency programs, resources and outreach activities. GAO-11-548R (Washington, D.C.: June 15, 2011).

[a]We identified 13 federal agencies that have mentor-protégé programs: the Department of Homeland Security, Department of Defense, Department of Energy, Department of State, Environmental Protection Agency, Federal Aviation Administration, General Services Administration, Department of Health and Human Services, National Aeronautics and Space Administration, Small Business Administration, Department of the Treasury, United States Agency for International Development, and Department of Veterans Affairs. See GAO, Mentor-Protégé Programs Have Polices That Aim to Benefit Participants but Do Not Require Postagreement Tracking,

[b]Bundling of contract requirements means the consolidation of two or more procurement requirements for goods or services previously provided or performed under separate smaller contracts into a solicitation of offers for a single contract that is likely to be unsuitable for award to a small business concern for various reasons. 15 U.S.C. § 632(o).

# Appendix IV: Potential Applicability of the Limited English Proficiency Executive Order to Federal Contracting

Executive Order 13,166, *Improving Access to Services for Persons with Limited English Proficiency*, issued on August 11, 2000, requires federal agencies to prepare a plan to improve access to federally conducted programs and activities for those with limited English proficiency (LEP).[1] Under the order, federal agencies must take reasonable steps to provide meaningful access to persons with LEP for federally conducted programs and activities. In addition, the Department of Justice (DOJ) serves as a central repository for agency plans to address LEP and provides guidance to agencies for developing such plans.

According to DOJ guidance issued on August 16, 2000 and available at LEP.GOV, the four factors to be considered in determining what constitutes "reasonable steps to ensure meaningful access" include

1. the number or proportion of such individuals in the eligible population,
2. the frequency with which they come into contact with the program,
3. the importance of the service provided by the program, and (4) the resources available to the recipients. In May 2011, DOJ also issued a Language Access Assessment and Planning Tool for Federally Conducted and Federally Assisted Programs to provide guidance to recipients of federal financial assistance and federal agencies. The first step in the assessment tool is a self-assessment that determines what type of contact an agency has with the LEP population and describes the elements that are part of effective language access policy directives and implementation plans.

DOJ officials told us that Executive Order 13,166 regarding LEP generally applied to outreach activities associated with federal contracting. The officials added that DOJ had not issued specific guidance related to the order on outreach to minority-owned businesses seeking to contract with the federal government. In addition, the planning tool does not provide guidance on outreach activities associated with federal contracting. According to DOJ officials,

> "Generally, current practice with regard to announcing federal government contracts and grants would not be altered under the Executive Order. In determining what is required, the focus of the analysis in this situation is on the first factor—the number or proportion of eligible LEP persons. Except, perhaps, in territories, it is reasonable to expect that the number or proportion of eligible contract or grant recipients who are LEP and are themselves attempting to find and respond to announcements of grants and contracts is negligible."

Federal agency officials and advocacy groups we spoke with cited linguistic barriers as a challenge on a limited basis. In addition, few agencies had taken action to address possible linguistic barriers, and most told us that they had not taken such action because they had not encountered this challenge. For example, based on its efforts as of July 2012, GSA found that only one region reported significant contact with persons with LEP.

## End Notes

[1] Socially disadvantaged individuals are those who have been subjected to racial or ethnic prejudice or cultural bias because of their identity as a member of a group without regard to their individual qualities. Economically disadvantaged individuals are those socially disadvantaged individuals whose ability to compete in the free enterprise system has been impaired due to diminished capital and credit opportunities compared with others in the same business area who are not socially disadvantaged. 15 U.S.C.A. § 637(a)(5),(6). Federal agencies generally do not use the term minority-owned business or refer to the racial classification of the business owner. In Adarand Constructors, Inc. v. Pena, the Supreme Court held that all federal programs—including those concerning federal contracting—that use racial classifications are subject to strict judicial scrutiny. To meet this standard, a program must be shown to meet a compelling governmental interest and must be narrowly tailored to meet that interest. 515 U.S. 200, 227 (1995).

[2] 15 U.S.C. § 644(g). The Small Business Act defines various socioeconomic categories of businesses. Small businesses are those that are independently owned and operated and are not dominant in their field of operations. 15 U.S.C. § 632(a). Women-owned small businesses must have at least 51 percent female ownership and the management and daily operations of the concern must be controlled by women. 15 U.S.C. § 632(n). Veteran-owned small businesses must be owned—also at least 51 percent—by one or more veterans and veterans must control the management and daily business operations. Service-disabled veteran-owned small businesses are veteran-owned small businesses owned and controlled by service-disabled veterans. 15 U.S.C. § 632(q). Small disadvantaged businesses must be owned and controlled by socially and economically disadvantaged individuals—such as African Americans, Hispanic Americans, Asian Pacific Americans, Subcontinent Asian Americans, or Native Americans—or by an economically disadvantaged Indian tribe or

Native Hawaiian organization. These owners must have at least a 51 percent stake in the business. 15 U.S.C. § 637(a)(4)(A); 13 C.F.R. § 124.103. Qualified Historically Underutilized Business Zone (HUBZone) small businesses must have their principal offices physically located in these historically underutilized business zones, which include economically distressed metropolitan or nonmetropolitan areas—that is, areas with low-income levels or high unemployment rates—and must employ some staff who live in these zones. 15 U.S.C. § 632(p).The small business regulations implementing the Small Business Act further define the size of these businesses. 13 C.F.R. §§ 121.401–121.413.

[3] U.S. Census Bureau, 2007 Survey of Business Owners.

[4] In its annual report on small business procurement goals, SBA excludes certain contract dollars when calculating percentages of dollars obligated to small businesses. The primary justification for these exclusions is that these contracts are not subject to the Federal Acquisition Regulation. According to SBA, the total amount of contract dollars less these exclusions was $423 billion in fiscal year 2011. To view reports on these goals and exclusions see https://www.fpds.gov/fpdsng_cms/index.php/reports/63-small-business-goaling-report.

[5] FPDS-NG is the only government-wide system for obtaining information on how federal contract funds are being spent. Contracting obligation data are collected in FPDS-NG, a comprehensive, web-based tool and database that functions as a clearinghouse of information for all federal contract actions, including noncompetitive and competitive actions exceeding $3,000. FPDS-NG captures data on minority-owned businesses for the following groups: Asian-Pacific American, Subcontinent Asian (Asian-Indian) American, Black American, Hispanic American, Native American, and has a category for other groups. Businesses that self-identity as minority-owned do so when registering with the Central Contractor Registration (CCR)—the primary registrant database for contracting with the federal government. As part of the registration process, businesses have the option of designating themselves as minority-owned to indicate that the firm is 51-percent owned and the management and daily operations are controlled by one or more members of the selected socioeconomic groups mentioned above. When contract funds are obligated, the business information is transferred to FPDS-NG. CCR migrated to the System for Award Management (SAM) on July 29, 2012. The General Services Administration (GSA) is consolidating the government-wide acquisition and award system into SAM, a free website which is being developed in phases. Phase 1, released in July 2012, includes the capabilities found in CCR, Online Representations and Certifications Application, and the Extended Parties List System. Over the coming years, additional system migrations will be completed.

[6] 15 U.S.C. § 644(k). At DOD and many of its components, this office is referred to as the Office of Small Business Programs. For simplicity, we use the term OSDBU throughout the report.

[7] The purpose of our sampling approach was to identify agency officials who may have experience with the challenges that small, minority-owned businesses may face rather than to develop a random sample that would be suitable for making estimates of how often such challenges are encountered.

[8] 15 U.S.C. § 644(g). Goals are not set for specific racial and ethnic groups. The 23 percent goal and various subgoals for socioeconomic categories are statutory minimums.

[9] MBDA serves enterprises that are owned or controlled by one or more socially or economically disadvantaged persons from the following groups: African Americans; Puerto Ricans; Spanish-speaking Americans; Asian Pacific Americans; Native Americans; Eskimos; Aleuts; Asian Indians; and Hasidic Jewish Americans. See 15 C.F.R. §§ 1400.1. Additional

groups may apply to MBDA for a socially or economically disadvantaged designation. 15 C.F.R. §§ 1400.3 to 1400.6. MBDA is considering a petition to designate Arab-Americans as a socially or economically disadvantaged group. 77 Fed. Reg. 31,765 (May 30, 2012); 77 Fed. Reg. 46,346 (Aug. 3, 2012); 77 Fed. Reg. 53,780 (Sept. 4, 2012).

[10] The regulations governing participation in the SBA 8(a) Business Development Program include a rebuttable presumption that Black Americans, Hispanic Americans, Native Americans, Asian Pacific Americans, and Subcontinent Asian Americans are socially disadvantaged. Other groups may petition SBA for designation as socially disadvantaged under the 8(a) Program, and individuals who are not a member of a group presumed to be socially disadvantaged may establish that they are socially disadvantaged by a "preponderance of evidence." 13 C.F.R. § 124.103.

[11] Under certain conditions, the Department of Defense, United States Coast Guard, and National Aeronautics and Space Administration are authorized to contract without providing for full and open competition. 10 U.S.C. § 2304(c). Other executive agencies are provided similar authority under 41 U.S.C. § 3304.

[12] See 13 C.F.R. § 125.2(b)-(c); 13 C.F.R. § 125.3(e).

[13] The purpose of small business set-asides is to award certain acquisitions exclusively to small business concerns. A "set-aside for small business" is the reserving of an acquisition exclusively for participation by small business concerns. A small business set-aside may be open to all small businesses. A small business set-aside of a single acquisition or a class of acquisitions may be total or partial. 48 C.F.R. § 19.501(a).

[14] U.S.C. § 632(o).15 U.S.C. § 631(j).To foster the participation of small businesses in the contract opportunities of the federal government, federal agencies, to the maximum extent practical, are to avoid unnecessary and unjustified bundling of contract requirements that preclude small business participation in procurements as prime contractors.

[15] 15 U.S.C. §644(k).

[16] Under section 15(k)(10), the OSDBU director is to make recommendations regarding whether a particular contract should be awarded to a small business under certain programs designed to promote contracting opportunities for small businesses.

[17] See http://www.sba.gov/gcclassroom.

[18] 48 C.F.R. § 1.102(b). Past performance means an offeror's or contractor's performance on active and physically completed contracts.

[19] Different rules apply based on the type of contracting involved. For example, when engaged in a source selection for a contract by negotiation, past performance must be evaluated when the contract is expected to exceed the simplified acquisition threshold (unless a documented reason is provided). 48 C.F.R. § 15.304(c)(3).

[20] See 48 C.F.R. § 15.305(a)(2)(iv). The FAR states that offerors without a record of relevant past performance may not be evaluated favorably or unfavorably on past performance—in other words, they must be given a neutral rating for the past performance evaluation factor.

[21] A bid protest is a challenge to the award or proposed award of a contract for the procurement of goods and services or a challenge to the terms of a solicitation for such a contract. Bid protests may be filed at GAO against procurement actions by federal government agencies and can also be filed with the agency responsible for the procurement, and with the U.S. Court of Federal Claims. In addition, size and status protests based on business determinations can be filed with SBA.

[22] The Small Business Jobs Act of 2010 requires prime contractors on covered contracts to notify the contracting officer in writing if the prime contractor fails to use a small business concern as described in the prime contractor's bid or proposal or when a payment to a

subcontractor is reduced or 90 days or more past due. Pub. L. No. 111-240, §§ 1322, 1334, 124 Stat. 2504, 2540–2544 (2010). SBA has issued a proposed rule regarding these requirements. 76 Fed. Reg. 61,626 (Oct. 5, 2011).

[23] GAO, Improvements Needed to Help Ensure Reliability of SBA's Performance Data on Procurement Center Representatives, GAO-11-549R (Washington, D.C.: June 15, 2011).

[24] U.S. Department of Commerce, Minority Business Development Agency, Disparities in Capital Access between Minority and Non-Minority-Owned Businesses: The Troubling Reality of Capital Limitations Faced by MBEs (Washington, D.C.: 2010).

[25] A surety bond is form of insurance that guarantees contract completion.

[26] See appendix IV for a discussion of the potential applicability of Executive Order 13,166, Improving Access to Services for Persons with Limited English Proficiency, to federal contracting and outreach activities.

[27] GAO, Small Business Contracting: Action Needed by Those Agencies Whose Advocates Do Not Report to Agency Heads as Required, GAO-11-418 (Washington, D.C.: June 3, 2011).

[28] 15 U.S.C. § 644(h).

[29] Exec. Order No. 11,625, Prescribing Additional Arrangements for Developing and Coordinating a National Program for Minority Business Enterprise, 36 Fed. Reg. 19,967 (Oct. 13, 1971).

[30] The three quantitative measures are weighted and assigned different percentages. Prime contracting achievement equals 80 percent, subcontracting achievement 10 percent, and the agency's progress plan for meeting its goals 10 percent, for a total of 100 percent. SBA changed the scorecard methodology in fiscal year 2009, moving from a color-based methodology that used three potential grade ranges (green, yellow, red) to letter grades, with six potential grade ranges (A+, A, B, C, D, F). According to SBA, expanding the number of grade ranges allows for a clearer distinction among different agencies' performance. In addition, SBA incorporated two measurements—subcontracting and plan performance—that help explain the totality of an agency's small business efforts. There are nine plan progress elements, including demonstrating top-level agency commitment to small business contracting and implementing a strategy to increase the number of competitively awarded contracts to small businesses. Previous scorecards only addressed prime contracting achievement and did not offer an overall grade to assess agencies' comprehensive procurement practices.

[31] MBDA defines the dollar value of transactions as the total principal value of approved loans, equity financings, bonds, leases (property and equipment), assets under management, or other binding financial agreements secured by clients of the project. Further, eligible financial transactions are those that have a specific dollar value that expands a client's capital base and operations or produces some other direct commercial benefit.

[32] The Business Opportunity Development Reform Act of 1988 requires that SBA report the race or ethnicity, and gender, of business owners that participate in the 8(a) program. 15 U.S.C. 636(j)(16)(B)(iv).

[33] The OSDBU Council is an informal organization led by the OSDBU directors, who work with SBA and other stakeholders on federal small business contracting programs. The OSDBU Council also discusses and exchanges information on outreach events with small businesses to assist agencies in their small business contracting efforts.

## End Notes for Appendix I

[1] We did not include all programs and resources that provide government contracting assistance and information to minority-owned businesses.

[2] The purpose of our sampling approach was to identify agency officials who may have experience with the challenges faced by small, minority owned businesses. Because we did not use a random sample, findings cannot be generalized and may not represent the entire population of small, minority owned businesses.

In: Government Contracts …
Editor: Gregor Meijir

ISBN: 978-1-62618-713-9
© 2013 Nova Science Publishers, Inc.

*Chapter 2*

# THE "8(A) PROGRAM" FOR SMALL BUSINESSES OWNED AND CONTROLLED BY THE SOCIALLY AND ECONOMICALLY ISADVANTAGED: LEGAL REQUIREMENTS AND ISSUES*

*Kate M. Manuel and John R. Luckey*

## SUMMARY

Commonly known as the "8(a) Program," the Minority Small Business and Capital Ownership Development Program is one of several federal contracting programs for small businesses. The 8(a) Program provides participating small businesses with training, technical assistance, and contracting opportunities in the form of set-asides and sole-source awards. A "set-aside" is an acquisition in which only certain contractors may compete, while a sole-source award is a contract awarded, or proposed for award, without competition. In FY2011, the federal government spent $16.7 billion on contracts and subcontracts with 8(a) firms. Other programs provide similar assistance to other types of small businesses (e.g., women-owned, HUBZone).

* This is an edited, reformatted and augmented version of a Congressional Research Service publication, CRS Report for Congress R40744, from www.crs.gov, prepared for Members and Committees of Congress, dated January 4, 2013.

Eligibility for the 8(a) Program is generally limited to small businesses "unconditionally owned and controlled by one or more socially and economically disadvantaged individuals who are of good character and citizens of the United States" that demonstrate "potential for success." Each of these terms is further defined by the Small Business Act, regulations promulgated by the Small Business Administration (SBA), and judicial and administrative decisions.

A "business" is generally a for-profit entity that has a place of business located in the United States and operates primarily within the United States or makes a significant contribution to the U.S. economy by paying taxes or using American products, materials, or labor. A business is "small" if it is independently owned and operated; is not dominant in its field of operations; and meets any definitions or standards established by the Administrator of Small Business. Ownership is "unconditional" when it is not subject to any conditions precedent or subsequent, executory agreements, or similar limitations. "Control" is not the same as ownership and includes both strategic policy setting and day-to-day administration of business operations.

Members of certain racial and ethnic groups are presumed to be socially disadvantaged, although individuals who do not belong to these groups may prove they are also socially disadvantaged. To be economically disadvantaged, an individual must have a net worth of less than $250,000 (excluding ownership in the 8(a) firm and equity in one's primary residence) at the time of entry into the 8(a) Program. This amount increases to $750,000 for continuing eligibility. In determining whether an applicant has good character, SBA looks for criminal conduct, violations of SBA regulations, or current debarment or suspension from federal contracting. For a firm to have demonstrated "potential for success," it generally must have been in business in the field of its primary industry classification for at least two years immediately prior to applying to the 8(a) Program. However, small businesses owned by Indian tribes, Alaska Native Corporations (ANCs), Native Hawaiian Organizations (NHOs), and Community Development Corporations (CDCs) are eligible for the 8(a) Program under somewhat different terms.

The 8(a) Program has periodically been challenged on the grounds that the presumption that members of certain racial and ethnic groups are disadvantaged violates the constitutional guarantee of equal protection. The outcomes in early challenges to the program varied, with some courts finding that plaintiffs lacked standing because they were not economically disadvantaged. Most recently, a federal district court found that the program is not unconstitutional on its face because "breaking down barriers to minority business development created by discrimination" constituted a compelling government interest, and the government had a strong basis in evidence for concluding that race-based action was necessary to further this interest. However, the court found that the program was unconstitutional as applied in the military simulation and training industry because there was no evidence of public- or private-sector discrimination in this industry.

## INTRODUCTION

Commonly known as the “8(a) Program,” the Minority Small Business and Capital Ownership Development Program is one of several federal contracting programs for small businesses.[1] The 8(a) Program provides participating small businesses with training, technical assistance, and contracting opportunities in the form of set-asides and sole-source awards. A “set-aside” is an acquisition in which only certain contractors may compete, while a sole-source award is a contract awarded, or proposed for award, without competition. Eligibility for the 8(a) Program is generally limited to small businesses “unconditionally owned and controlled by one or more socially and economically disadvantaged individuals who are of good character and citizens of the United States” that demonstrate “potential for success.” However, small businesses owned by Indian tribes, Alaska Native Corporations (ANCs), Native Hawaiian Organizations (NHOs), and Community Development Corporations (CDCs) are eligible for the 8(a) Program under somewhat different terms. In FY2011, the federal government spent $16.7 billion on contracts and subcontracts with 8(a) firms.[2] Other programs provide similar assistance to other types of small businesses (e.g., women-owned, HUBZone).

The 8(a) and other programs for small businesses are of perennial interest to Congress, given that:

> It is the declared policy of the Congress that the Government should aid, counsel, assist, and protect, insofar as is possible, the interests of small-business concerns in order to preserve free competitive enterprise, to insure that a fair proportion of the total purchases and contracts or subcontracts for property and services for the Government (including but not limited to contracts or subcontracts for maintenance, repair, and construction) be placed with small-business enterprises, to insure that a fair proportion of the total sales of Government property be made to such enterprises, and to maintain and strengthen the overall economy of the Nation.[3]

However, recent Congresses have had particular interest in the 8(a) Program because of the recession of 2007-2009,[4] its effects on minority-owned small businesses,[5] and small businesses' role in job creation.[6]

This report provides a brief history of the 8(a) Program, summarizes key requirements, and discusses legal challenges alleging that the program's presumption that members of certain racial and ethnic groups are socially disadvantaged violates the constitutional guarantee of equal protection.

# HISTORICAL DEVELOPMENT

## Origins of the 8(a) Program

The current 8(a) Program resulted from the merger of two distinct types of federal programs: those seeking to assist small businesses in general and those seeking to assist racial and ethnic minorities. This merger first occurred, as a matter of executive branch practice, in 1967 and was given a statutory basis in 1978.

### *Federal Programs for Small Businesses*

Congress first authorized a federal agency to enter into prime contracts with other agencies and subcontract with small businesses for the performance of these contracts in 1942. The agency was the Smaller War Plants Corporation (SWPC), which was created partly for this purpose, and Congress gave it these powers in order to ameliorate small businesses' financial difficulties while also "mobiliz[ing] the productive facilities of small business in the interest of successful prosecution of the war."[7] The SWPC's subcontracting authority expired along with the SWPC at the end of the World War II. However, in 1951, at the start of the Korean War, Congress created the Small Defense Plants Administration (SDPA), which was generally given the same powers that the SWPC had exercised.[8] Two years later, in 1953, Congress transferred the SDPA's subcontracting authorities, among others, to the newly created Small Business Administration,[9] with the intent that the SBA would exercise these powers in peacetime, as well as in wartime.[10] When the Small Business Act of 1958 transformed the SBA into a permanent independent agency, this subcontracting authority was included in Section 8(a) of the act.[11] At its inception, the SBA's subcontracting authority was not limited to small businesses owned and controlled by the socially and economically disadvantaged. Under the original Section 8(a), the SBA could contract with any "small-business concerns or others,"[12] but the SBA seldom, if ever, employed this subcontracting authority, focusing instead upon its loan and other programs.[13]

### *Federal Programs for Minorities*

Federal programs for minorities began developing at approximately the same time as those for small businesses, although there was initially no explicit overlap between them. The earliest programs were created by executive orders, beginning with President Franklin Roosevelt's order on June 25, 1941, requiring that all federal agencies include a clause in defense-related contracts prohibiting contractors from discriminating on the basis of race, creed, color, or national origin.[14] Subsequent Presidents followed Roosevelt's example, issuing a number of executive orders seeking to improve the employment opportunities of "Negroes, Spanish-Americans, Orientals, Indians, Jews, Puerto Ricans, etc."[15] These executive branch initiatives took on new importance after the Kerner Commission's report on the causes of the urban riots of 1966 concluded that African Americans would need "special encouragement" to enter the economic mainstream.[16]

Presidents Lyndon Johnson and Richard Nixon laid the foundations for the present 8(a) Program in the hope of providing such "encouragement." Johnson created the President's Test Cities Program (PTCP), which involved a small-scale use of the SBA's authority under Section 8(a) to award contracts to firms willing to locate in urban areas and hire unemployed individuals, largely African Americans, or sponsor minority-owned businesses by providing capital or management assistance.[17] However, under the PTCP, small businesses did not have to be minority-owned to receive subcontracts under Section 8(a).[18]

Nixon's program was larger and focused more specifically on minority-owned small businesses.[19] During the Nixon Administration, the SBA promulgated its earliest regulations for the 8(a) Program. In 1970, the first of these regulations articulated the SBA's policy of using Section 8(a) to "assist small concerns owned by disadvantaged persons to become self-sufficient, viable businesses capable of competing effectively in the market place."[20] A later regulation, promulgated in 1973, defined "disadvantaged persons" as including, but not limited to, "black Americans, Spanish-Americans, oriental Americans, Eskimos, and Aleuts."[21]

However, the SBA lacked explicit statutory authority for focusing its 8(a) Program on minority-owned businesses until 1978,[22] although courts generally rejected challenges alleging that SBA's implementation of the program was unauthorized because it was "not specifically mentioned in statute."[23]

### *1978 Amendments to the Small Business Act and Subsequent Regulations*

In 1978, Congress amended the Small Business Act to give the SBA statutory authority for its 8(a) Program for minority-owned businesses.[24] Under the 1978 amendments, SBA can only subcontract under Section 8(a) with "socially and economically disadvantaged small business concerns,"[25] or businesses which are least 51% owned by one or more socially and economically disadvantaged individuals and whose management and daily operations are controlled by such individual(s).[26]

The 1978 amendments established a basic definition of "socially disadvantaged individuals," which included those who have been "subjected to racial or ethnic prejudice or cultural bias because of their identity as a member of a group without regard to their individual qualities."[27] They also included congressional findings that "Black Americans, Hispanic Americans, Native Americans, and other minorities" are socially disadvantaged.[28] Thus, if an individual was a member of one of these groups, he or she was presumed to be socially disadvantaged.

Otherwise, the amendments granted the SBA broad discretion to recognize additional groups or individuals as socially disadvantaged based upon criteria promulgated in regulations.[29] Under these regulations, which include a three-part test for determining whether minority groups not mentioned in the amendment's findings are disadvantaged,[30] the SBA recognized the racial or ethnic groups listed in *Table 1* as socially disadvantaged for purposes of the 8(a) Program.[31]

The regulations also established standards of evidence to be met by individuals demonstrating personal disadvantage and procedures for rebutting the presumption of social disadvantage accorded to members of recognized minority groups.[32]

The 1978 amendments also defined "economically disadvantaged individuals," for purposes of the 8(a) Program, as "those socially disadvantaged individuals whose ability to compete in the free enterprise system has been impaired ... as compared to others in the same business area who are not socially disadvantaged."[33] Later, the SBA established by regulation that personal net worth of less than $250,000 at the time of entry into the 8(a) Program ($750,000 for continuing eligibility) constitutes economic disadvantage.[34]

**Table 1. Groups Presumed to Be Socially Disadvantaged**

| Group | Countries of Origin Included Within Group |
|---|---|
| Black Americans | n/a |
| Hispanic Americans | n/a |
| Native Americans (including American Indians, Eskimos, Aleuts, Native Hawaiians) | n/a |
| Asian Pacific Americans | Burma, Thailand, Malaysia, Indonesia, Singapore, Brunei, Japan, China (including Hong Kong), Taiwan, Laos, Cambodia, Vietnam, Korea, The Philippines, U.S. Trust Territory of the Pacific Islands (Republic of Palau), Republic of the Marshall Islands, Federated States of Micronesia, Commonwealth of the Northern Mariana Islands, Guam, Samoa, Macao, Fiji, Tonga, Kiribati, Tuvalu, Nauru |
| Subcontinent Asian Americans | India, Pakistan, Bangladesh, Sri Lanka, Bhutan, the Maldives Islands, Nepal |

Source: Congressional Research Service, based on 13 C.F.R. §124.103(b).

## Expansion of the 8(a) Program to Include "Disadvantaged" Groups

Although the 8(a) Program was originally established for the benefit of disadvantaged *individuals*, in the 1980s, Congress expanded the program to include small businesses owned by four "disadvantaged" *groups*.

The first owner-group to be included was Community Development Corporations (CDCs). A CDC is:

> a nonprofit organization responsible to residents of the area it serves which is receiving financial assistance under part 1 [42 USCS §§9805 et seq.] and any organization more than 50 percent of which is owned by such an organization, or otherwise controlled by such an organization, or designated by such an organization for the purpose of this subchapter [42 USCS §§9801 et seq.].[35]

Congress created CDCs with the Community Development Act of 1981[36] and instructed the SBA to issue regulations ensuring that CDCs could participate in the 8(a) Program.[37]

In 1986, two additional owner-groups, Indian tribes and Alaska Native Corporations, became eligible for the 8(a) Program when Congress passed legislation providing that firms owned by Indian tribes, which included Alaskan Native Corporations (ANCs),[38] were to be deemed "socially disadvantaged" for purposes of the 8(a) Program.[39] In 1992, ANCs were further deemed to be "economically disadvantaged."[40]

The final owner-group, that of Native Hawaiian Organizations (NHOs), was recognized in 1988.[41]

An NHO was defined as:

> any community service organization serving Native Hawaiians in the State of Hawaii which—
>
> A. is a nonprofit corporation that has filed articles of incorporation with the director (or the designee thereof) of the Hawaii Department of Commerce and Consumer Affairs, or any successor agency,
> B. is controlled by Native Hawaiians, and
> C. whose business activities will principally benefit such Native Hawaiians.[42]

## Current Requirements

Under the current 8(a) Program, participating firms are eligible for set-asides or sole-source awards of federal contracts, as well as training and technical assistance from SBA.

Detailed statutory and regulatory requirements govern eligibility for the Program; set-asides and sole-source awards to 8(a) firms; and related issues. These requirements are generally the same for all participants in the 8(a) Program, although there are instances where there are "special rules" for 8(a) firms owned by groups.[43]

An *Appendix* compares the requirements applicable to individual owners of 8(a) firms to those applicable to groups owning 8(a) firms (i.e., Alaska Native Corporations, Indian tribes, Native Hawaiian Organizations, and Community Development Corporations).[44]

## Requirements in General

### *Eligibility for the 8(a) Program*

Eligibility for the 8(a) Program is limited to "small business[es] which [are] unconditionally owned and controlled by one or more socially and economically disadvantaged individuals who are of good character and citizens of and residing in the United States, and which demonstrate potential for success."[45] Each of these terms is further defined by the Small Business Act; regulations that the SBA has promulgated to implement Section 8(a); and judicial and administrative decisions.[46] The eligibility requirements are the same at the time of entry into the 8(a) Program and throughout the Program unless otherwise noted.[47]

### *"Business"*

Except for small agricultural cooperatives, a "business" is a for-profit entity that has a place of business located in the United States and operates primarily within the United States or makes a significant contribution to the U.S. economy by paying taxes or using American products, materials, or labor.[48] For purposes of the 8(a) Program, businesses may take the form of individual proprietorships, partnerships, limited liability companies, corporations, joint ventures, associations, trusts, or cooperatives.[49]

### *"Small"*

A business is "small" if it is independently owned and operated; is not dominant in its field of operations; and meets any definitions or standards established by the Administrator of the SBA.[50] These standards focus primarily upon the size of the business as measured by the number of employees or its gross income, but they also take into account the size of other businesses within the same industry.[51] For example, businesses in the field of "scheduled passenger air transportation" are "small" if they have fewer than 1,500 employees, while those in the data processing field are "small" if they have a gross income of less than $25 million.[52]

Affiliations between businesses, or relationships allowing one party control or the power of control over another,[53] generally count in size determinations, with the SBA considering "the receipts, employees, or other measure of size of the concern whose size is at issue and all of its domestic and foreign affiliates, regardless of whether the affiliates are organized for profit."[54] Businesses can thus be determined to be other than small because of their involvement in joint ventures,[55] subcontracting arrangements,[56] or franchise or license agreements,[57] among other things, provided that their income or personnel numbers, plus those of their affiliate(s), are over the pertinent size threshold.

### *"Unconditionally Owned and Controlled"*

Participants in the 8(a) Program must be "at least 51% unconditionally and directly owned by one or more socially and economically disadvantaged individuals who are citizens of the United States" unless they are owned by an Indian tribe, Alaska Native Corporation (ANC), Native Hawaiian Organization (NHO), or Community Development Corporation (CDC).[58] Ownership is "unconditional" when it is not subject to any conditions precedent or subsequent, executory agreements, voting trusts, restrictions on assignment of voting rights, or other arrangements that could cause the benefits of ownership to go to another entity.[59] Ownership is "direct" when the disadvantaged individuals own the business in their own right and not through an intermediary (e.g., ownership by another business entity or by a trust that is owned and controlled by one or more disadvantaged individuals).[60] Non-disadvantaged individuals and non-participant businesses that own at least 10% of an 8(a) business may generally own no more than 10 to 20% of any other 8(a) firm.[61] Non-participant businesses that earn the majority of their revenue in the same or similar line of business are likewise barred from owning more than 10 to 20% of another 8(a) firm.[62]

Participants must also be controlled by one or more disadvantaged individuals.[63] "Control is not the same as ownership" and includes both strategic policy setting and day-to-day management and administration of business operations.[64] Management and daily business operations must also be conducted by one or more disadvantaged individuals unless the 8(a) business is owned by an Indian tribe, ANC, NHO, or CDC.[65] These individuals must have managerial experience "of the extent and complexity needed to run the concern" and generally must devote themselves full-time to the business "during the normal working hours of firms in the same or similar line of business."[66]

A disadvantaged individual must hold the highest officer position within the business.[67] Non-disadvantaged individuals may otherwise be involved in the management of an 8(a) business, or may be stockholders, partners, limited liability members, officers, or directors of an 8(a) business.[68] However, they may not exercise actual control or have power to control, or receive compensation greater than that of the highest-paid officer without SBA approval.[69]

### *"Socially Disadvantaged Individual"*

Socially disadvantaged individuals are "those who have been subjected to racial or ethnic prejudice or cultural bias within American society because of their identities as members of groups and without regard to their individual qualities."[70] Members of designated groups, listed in *Table 1*, are entitled to a rebuttable presumption of social disadvantage for purposes of the 8(a) Program,[71] although this presumption can be overcome with "credible evidence to the contrary."[72] Individuals who are not members of designated groups must prove they are socially disadvantaged by a preponderance of the evidence.[73] Such individuals must show (1) at least one objective distinguishing feature that has contributed to social disadvantage (e.g., race, ethnic origin, gender, physical handicap, long-term residence in an environment isolated from mainstream American society); (2) personal experiences of substantial and chronic social disadvantage in American society; and (3) negative impact on entry into or advancement in the business world.[74]

In assessing the third factor, the SBA will consider all relevant evidence produced by the applicant, but must consider the applicant's education, employment, and business history to see if the totality of the circumstances shows disadvantage.[75]

Groups not included in *Table 1* may obtain listing by demonstrating disadvantage by a preponderance of the evidence.[76]

### *"Economically Disadvantaged Individual"*

Economically disadvantaged individuals are "socially disadvantaged individuals whose ability to compete in the free enterprise system has been impaired due to diminished financial capital and credit opportunities as compared to others in the same or similar line of business who are not socially disadvantaged."[77]

Individuals claiming economic disadvantage must describe it in a personal statement and submit financial documentation.[78] The SBA will examine their personal income for the past three years, their personal net worth, and the fair market value of the assets they own.[79]

However, principal ownership in a prospective or current 8(a) business is generally excluded when calculating net worth, as is equity in individuals' primary residence.80 For initial eligibility, applicants to the 8(a) Program must have a net worth of less than $250,000.[81] For continued eligibility, net worth must be less than $750,000.[82]

### *"Good Character"*

In determining whether an applicant to, or participant in, the 8(a) Program possesses "good character," the SBA looks for criminal conduct; violations of SBA regulations; current debarment or suspension from government contracting; managers or key employees who lack business integrity; and the knowing submission of false information to the SBA.[83]

### *"Demonstrated Potential for Success"*

For a firm to have demonstrated potential for success, it generally must have been in business in the field of its primary industry classification for at least two full years immediately prior to the date of its application to the 8(a) Program.[84] However, the SBA may grant a waiver allowing firms that have been in business for less than two years to enter the 8(a) Program when (1) the disadvantaged individuals upon whom eligibility is based have substantial business management experience; (2) the business has demonstrated the technical experience necessary to carry out its business plan with a substantial likelihood of success; (3) the firm has adequate capital to sustain its operations and carry out its business plan; (4) the firm has a record of successful performance on contracts in its primary field of operations; and (5) the firm presently has, or can demonstrate its ability to timely obtain, the personnel, facilities, equipment, and other resources necessary to perform contracts under Section 8(a).[85]

### *Set-Asides and Sole-Source Awards Under Section 8(a)*

Section 8(a) of the Small Business Act authorizes agencies to award contracts for goods or services, or to perform construction work, to the SBA for subcontracting to small businesses participating in the 8(a) Program.[86] A "set-aside" is an acquisition in which only certain contractors may compete, while a sole-source award is a contract awarded, or proposed for award, without competition.[87] Although the Competition in Contracting Act (CICA) generally requires that agencies obtain "full and open competition through the use of competitive procedures" when procuring goods or services, set-asides and sole-source awards are both permissible under CICA. In fact, an 8(a) set-aside is a recognized competitive procedure.[88] Agencies are effectively encouraged to subcontract through the 8(a) Program because there are government-wide and agency-specific goals regarding the percentage of procurement dollars awarded to "small disadvantaged businesses," among others.[89] Awards made via set-asides or on a sole-source basis count toward these goals,[90] and businesses participating in the 8(a) Program are considered small disadvantaged businesses.[91]

### *Discretion to Subcontract Through the 8(a) Program*

There are few limits on agency discretion to subcontract through the 8(a) Program.[92] However, the SBA is prohibited by regulation from accepting procurements for award under Section 8(a) when

1) the procuring agency issued a solicitation for or otherwise expressed publicly a clear intent to reserve the procurement as a set-aside for small businesses not participating in the 8(a) Program prior to offering the requirement to SBA for award as an 8(a) contract;[93]
2) the procuring agency competed the requirement among 8(a) firms prior to offering the requirement to SBA and receiving SBA's acceptance of it;[94] or
3) the SBA makes a written determination that "acceptance of the procurement for 8(a) award would have an adverse impact on an individual small business, a group of small businesses located in a specific geographical location, or other small business programs."[95]

Additionally, SBA is barred from awarding an 8(a) contract, either via a set-aside or on a sole-source basis, "if the price of the contract results in a cost to the contracting agency which exceeds a fair market price."[96]

Otherwise, agency officials may offer contracts to the SBA "in [their] discretion," and the SBA may accept requirements for the 8(a) Program "whenever it determines such action is necessary or appropriate."[97] The courts and the Government Accountability Office (GAO) will generally not hear protests of agencies' determinations regarding whether to procure specific requirements through the 8(a) Program unless it can be shown that government officials acted in bad faith or contrary to federal law.[98]

### *Monetary Thresholds and Subcontracting Mechanism Under 8(a)*

Once the SBA has accepted a contract for the 8(a) Program, the contract is awarded either through a set-aside or on a sole-source basis, with the amount of the contract generally determining the acquisition method used, as *Figure 1* illustrates. When the anticipated total value of the contract, including any options, is less than $4 million ($6.5 million for manufacturing contracts), the contract is normally awarded without competition.[99] In contrast, when the anticipated value of the contract exceeds $4 million ($6.5 million for manufacturing contracts), the contract generally must be awarded via a set-aside with competition limited to 8(a) firms so long as there is a reasonable expectation that at least two eligible and responsible 8(a) firms will submit offers and the award can be made at fair market price.[100] Sole-source awards of contracts valued at $4 million ($6.5 million or more for manufacturing contracts) may only be made when (1) there is not a reasonable expectation that at least two eligible and responsible 8(a) firms will submit offers at a fair market price, or (2) the SBA accepts the requirement on behalf of an 8(a) firm owned by an Indian tribe, an ANC or, in the case of Department of Defense contracts, an NHO.[101] Requirements valued at more than $4 million ($6.5 million for manufacturing contracts) cannot be divided into several acquisitions at lesser amounts in order to make sole-source awards.[102]

Source: Congressional Research Service.

Figure 1. Acquisition Methods at Various Price Thresholds.

### *Other Requirements*

Other key requirements of the 8(a) Program include the following:

- *Inability to protest an 8(a) firm's eligibility for an award*: When the SBA makes or proposes an award to an 8(a) firm, that firm's eligibility for the award cannot be challenged or protested as part of the solicitation or proposed contract award. Instead, information concerning a firm'seligibility for the 8(a) Program must be submitted to SBA in accordance with separate requirements contained in 13 C.F.R. §124.517.[103]
- *Maximum of nine years in the 8(a) Program*: Firms may participate in the 8(a) Program for no more than nine years from the date of their admission into the Program, although they may be terminated or graduate from the program before nine years have passed.[104]
- *One-time eligibility for the 8(a) Program*: Once a firm or a disadvantaged individual upon whom a firm's eligibility was based

has exited the 8(a) Program after participating in it for any length of time, neither the firm nor the individual is generally eligible to participate in the 8(a) Program again.[105] When at least 50% of the assets of one firm are the same as those of another firm, the firms are considered identical for purposes of eligibility for the 8(a) Program.[106]

- *Limits on ownership of 8(a) firms by family members of current or former 8(a) firm owners*: Individuals generally may not use their disadvantaged status to qualify a firm for the 8(a) Program if the individual has an immediate family member who is using, or has used, his or her disadvantaged status to qualify a firm for the 8(a) Program.[107]
- *Limits on the amount of 8(a) contracts that a firm may receive*: 8(a) firms may generally not receive additional sole-source awards once they have received a combined total of competitive and sole-source awards in excess of $100 million, in the case of firms whose size is based on their number of employees, or in excess of an amount equivalent to the lesser of (1) $100 million or (2) five times the size standard for the industry, in the case of firms whose size is based on their revenues.[108] Additionally, 8(a) firms in the "transitional stage," or the last five years of participation, must achieve annual targets for the amount of revenues they receive from non-8(a) sources.[109] These targets increase over time, with firms required to attain 15% of their revenue from non-8(a) sources in the fifth year; 25% in the sixth year; 35% in the seventh year; 45% in the eight year; and 55% in the ninth year.[110] Firms that do not display the relevant percentages of revenue from non-8(a) sources are ineligible for sole-source 8(a) contracts "unless and until" they correct the situation.[111]
- *Limitations on subcontracting*: Although not only under the authority of Section 8(a) of the Small Business Act or applicable only to 8(a) businesses, limitations on subcontracting require that small businesses receiving contracts under a set-aside perform minimum percentages of the contract work.[112] These percentages vary depending upon the type of the contract, with employees of the small business required to perform (1) at least 50% of the personnel costs of service contracts; (2) at least 50% of the costs of manufacturing (excluding materials) in supply contacts; (3) at least 15% of the costs of construction (excluding materials) in general construction contracts; and (4) at least 25% of the costs of construction (excluding materials) in "special trade" construction contracts.[113]

## Requirements for Tribally, ANC-, NHO-, and CDC-Owned Firms

Tribes, ANCs, NHOs or CDCs themselves generally do not participate in the 8(a) Program. Rather, businesses that are at least 51% owned by such entities participate in the 8(a) Program,114 although the rules governing their participation are somewhat different from those for the 8(a) Program generally.[115]

### *Eligibility for the 8(a) Program*

#### "Small"

Firms owned by Indian tribes, ANCs, NHOs, and CDCs must be "small" under the SBA's size standards.116 However, certain affiliations with the owning entity or other business enterprises of that entity are excluded in size determinations unless the Administrator of Small Business determines that a small business owned by an Indian tribe, ANC, NHO, or CDC "[has] obtained, or [is] likely to obtain, a substantial unfair competitive advantage within an industry category" because of such exclusions.117 Other affiliations of small businesses owned by Indian tribes, ANCs, NHOs, or CDCs can count in size determinations, and ANC-owned firms, in particular, have been subjected to early graduation from the 8(a) Program because they exceeded the size standards.[118]

#### "Business"

Firms owned by Indian tribes, ANCs, NHOs, and CDCs must be "businesses" under the SBA's definition.[119] Although ANCs themselves may be for-profit or non-profit, ANC-owned businesses must be for-profit to participate in the 8(a) Program.[120]

#### "Unconditionally Owned and Controlled"

Firms owned by Indian tribes, ANCs, NHOs, and CDCs must be unconditionally owned and substantially controlled by the tribe, ANC, NHO, or CDC, respectively.[121] However, under SBA regulations, tribally or ANC-owned firms may be managed by individuals who are not members of the tribe or Alaska Natives if the firm can demonstrate:

> that the Tribe can hire and fire those individuals, that it will retain control of all management decisions common to boards of directors,

including strategic planning, budget approval, and the employment and compensation of officers, and that a written management development plan exists which shows how Tribal members will develop managerial skills sufficient to manage the concern or similar Tribally-owned concerns in the future.[122]

The rules governing NHO-owned firms do not address management of NHO-owned firms by persons who are not Native Hawaiians,[123] and although the general rules apply where no "special rules" exist,[124] it seems unlikely that NHO-owned firms are treated differently from tribally or ANC-owned firms in this regard. CDCs are to be managed and have their daily operations conducted by individuals with "managerial experience of an extent and complexity needed to run the [firm]."[125]

**"Socially Disadvantaged"**

As owners of prospective or current 8(a) firms, Indian tribes, ANCs, NHOs, and CDCs are all presumed to be socially disadvantaged.[126]

**"Economically Disadvantaged"**

By statute, ANCs are deemed to be economically disadvantaged,[127] and CDCs are similarly presumed to be economically disadvantaged.[128] Indian tribes and NHOs, in contrast, must establish economic disadvantage at least once.

Indian tribes must present data on, among other things, the number of tribe members; the tribal unemployment rate; the per capita income of tribe members; the percentage of the local Indian population above the poverty level; the tribe's access to capital; the tribe's assets as disclosed in current financial statements; and all businesses wholly or partially owned by tribal enterprises or affiliates, as well as their primary industry classification.[129] However, once a tribe has established that it is economically disadvantaged for purposes of one 8(a) business, it need not reestablish economic disadvantage in order to have other businesses certified for the 8(a) Program *unless* the Director of the Office of Business Development requires it to do so.[130]

When determining whether an NHO is economically disadvantaged, SBA will consider "the individual economic status of NHO's members," the majority of whom "must meet the same initial eligibility economic disadvantaged thresholds as individually-owned 8(a) applicants."[131] Specifically:

> For the first 8(a) applicant owned by a particular NHO, individual NHO members must meet the same initial eligibility economic disadvantage thresholds as individually-owned 8(a) applicants. For any additional 8(a) applicant owned by the NHO, individual NHO members must meet the economic disadvantage thresholds for continued 8(a) eligibility.[132]

### "Good Character"

When an organization owns an actual or prospective 8(a) firm, all members, officers, or employees of that organization are generally not required to show good character. The regulations governing tribally and ANC-owned firms explicitly address the issue, stating that the "good character" requirement applies only to officers or directors of the firm, or shareholders owning more than a 20% interest.[133] NHO-owned firms may be subject to the same requirements in practice.[134] With CDC-owned firms, the firm itself and "all of its principals" must have good character.[135]

### "Demonstrated Potential for Success"

Firms owned by ANCs, Indian tribes, NHOs, and CDCs may evidence "potential for success" in several ways, including by demonstrating that:

1) the firm has been in business for at least two years, as shown by individual or consolidated income tax returns for each of the two previous tax years showing operating revenues in the primary industry in which the firm seeks certification;
2) the individuals who will manage and control the daily operations of the firm have substantial technical and management experience; the firm has a record of successful performance on government or other contracts in its primary industry category; and the firm has adequate capital to sustain its operations and carry out its business plan; or
3) the owner-group has made a firm written commitment to support the operations of the firm and has the financial ability to do so.[136]

The first of these ways for demonstrating potential for success is the same for individually owned firms,[137] and the second arguably corresponds to the circumstances in which SBA may waive the requirement that individually owned firms have been in business for at least two years.[138]

There is no equivalent to the third way for individually owned firms, and some commentators have suggested that this provision could "benefit ANCs by allowing more expeditious and effortless access to 8(a) contracts for new concerns without having to staff new subsidiaries with experienced management."[139]

## Report of Benefits for Firms Owned By ANCs, Indian Tribes, NHOs, and CDCs

Although implementation of this requirement has been delayed,[140] 8(a) firms owned by ANCs, Indian tribes, NHOs, and CDCs must submit information annually to the SBA showing:

> how the Tribe, ANC, NHO or CDC has provided benefits to the Tribal or native members and/or the Tribal, native or other community due to the Tribe's/ANC's/NHO's/CDC's participation in the 8(a) ... program through one or more firms. This data includes information relating to funding cultural programs, employment assistance, jobs, scholarships, internships, subsistence activities, and other services provided by the Tribe, ANC, NHO or CDC to the affected community.[141]

### *Set-Asides and Sole-Source Awards*

Like other participants in the 8(a) Program, firms owned by Indian tribes, ANCs, NHOs, and CDCs are eligible for 8(a) set-asides and may receive sole-source awards valued at less than $4 million ($6.5 million for manufacturing contracts).

However, firms owned by Indian tribes and ANCs can also receive sole-source awards in excess of $4 million ($6.5 million for manufacturing contracts) even when contracting officers reasonably expect that that at least two eligible and responsible 8(a) firms will submit offers and the award can be made at fair market price.[142]

NHO-owned firms may receive sole-source awards from the Department of Defense under the same conditions.[143]

### *Other Requirements*

Firms owned by Indian tribes, ANCs, NHOs, and CDCs are governed by the same regulations as other 8(a) firms where certain of the "other requirements" are involved, including (1) inability to protest an 8(a) firm's eligibility for an award;[144] (2) maximum of nine years in the 8(a) Program (for individual firms);[145] and (3) limits on subcontracting.[146]

However, the requirements for such firms differ somewhat from those for other 8(a) firms where one-time eligibility for the 8(a) Program; limits on majority ownership of 8(a) firms; and limits on the amount of 8(a) contracts that a firm may receive are involved.

Firms owned by Indian tribes, ANCs, NHOs, and CDCs may participate in the 8(a) Program only one time.[147] However, unlike the disadvantaged individuals upon whom other firms' eligibility for the 8(a) Program is based, Indian tribes, ANCs, NHOs, and CDCs may confer eligibility for the 8(a) Program upon firms on multiple occasions and for an indefinite period.[148] Additionally, although Indian tribes, ANCs, NHOs, and CDCs may not own 51% or more of a firm obtaining the majority of its revenues from the same "primary" industry in which another firm they own or owned currently operates or has operated within the past two years, there are no limits on the number of firms they may own that operate in other primary industries.[149] Moreover, Indian tribes, ANCs, NHOs, and CDCs may own multiple firms that earn less than 50% of their revenue in the same "secondary" industries.[150]

Finally, firms owned by Indian tribes, ANCs, and NHOs may continue to receive additional sole-source awards even after they have received a combined total of competitive and sole-source 8(a) contracts in excess of the dollar amount set forth in 13 C.F.R. Section 124.519, while individually owned firms may not.[151]

However, firms owned by any of these four types of entities are subject to the same requirements regarding the percentages of revenue received from non-8(a) sources at various stages of their participation in the 8(a) Program as other 8(a) firms.[152]

## CONSTITUTIONALITY OF THE 8(A) PROGRAM

The 8(a) Program has periodically been challenged on the grounds that the presumption that members of certain racial and ethnic groups are disadvantaged violates the constitutional guarantee of equal protection. The outcomes in early challenges to the program varied, with some courts finding that the plaintiffs lacked standing to bring such challenges because they were not economically disadvantaged, or were otherwise ineligible for the program;[153] and other courts finding that the program was unconstitutional as applied in specific cases.[154]

Most recently, in *DynaLantic Corporation v. U.S. Department of Defense*, the U.S. District Court for the District of Columbia found that the 8(a) Program was not unconstitutional on its face because "breaking down barriers to minority business development created by discrimination" constituted a

compelling government interest, and the government had a strong basis in evidence for concluding that race-based action was necessary to further this interest.[155]

However, the court found that the program was unconstitutional as applied in the military simulation and training industry because the Department of Defense (DOD) conceded it had "no evidence of discrimination, either in the public or private sector, in the simulation and training industry."[156]

Particularly in its rejection of the facial challenge to the 8(a) Program, the court emphasized certain aspects of the program's history and requirements when finding that the government had articulated a compelling interest for the program and had a strong basis in evidence for its actions. Specifically, the court rejected the plaintiff's assertion that the 8(a) Program was "not truly remedial," but rather favored "virtually all minority groups ... over the larger pool of citizens," because non-minority individuals may qualify for the program, and all 8(a) applicants must demonstrate economic disadvantage.[157] The court also noted that the history of the 8(a) program prior to 1978 (when Congress expressly authorized set-asides for disadvantaged small businesses) had evidenced that race-neutral methods were insufficient to promote contracting with minority-owned small businesses.[158]

The court further noted that the 8(a) Program was intended to be a business development program, not a means to "channel contracts" to minority firms;[159] that Section 8(a) of the Small Business Act expressly provides that awards may be made through the 8(a) Program only when SBA determines that "such action is necessary and appropriate";[160] and that the act requires the President and SBA to report annually to Congress on the program, thereby ensuring that Congress has evidence as to whether there is a "continuing compelling need for the program."[161]

Similarly, in finding that the program was narrowly tailored to meet the government's interests, the court noted (1) that goals for contracting with small disadvantaged businesses are purely aspirational, and there are no penalties for failing to meet them;[162] (2) the nine-year limits on program participation for individual owners and firms;[163] and (3) that SBA may not accept a requirement for the 8(a) Program if it determines that doing so will have a adverse effect on another small business or group of small businesses.[164]

The court emphasized that the last two factors, in particular, helped ensure that race-conscious remedies do not "last longer than the discriminatory effects [they are] designed to eliminate,"[165] and "work the least harm possible to other innocent persons competing for the benefit."[166]

In contrast, in upholding the as-applied challenge, the court focused on the industry in which DOD had proposed using an 8(a) set-aside, rather than aspects of the 8(a) Program.

The court characterized the military simulation and training industry as a "highly skilled" one,[167] and noted that the government had conceded there was no evidence of public or private sector discrimination in this industry.[168]

The court further suggested that, with the requisite evidence, the government could use the 8(a) Program to make awards in the military simulation and training industry.[169]

However, despite such caveats, the 8(a) Program would appear vulnerable to as-applied challenges in the wake of the *DynaLantic* decision, particularly in other "highly skilled" industries where there could be questions about the availability of qualified minority contractors.[170]

As-applied challenges to the 8(a) Program have succeed in the past, arguably without materially diminishing the efficacy of the program.[171] The current situation could be different, though, in that competition for federal contracts seems likely to increase as federal procurement spending decreases due to budget cuts and, potentially, sequestration.[172]

Both parties in *DynaLantic* have appealed the district court's decision to the U.S. Court of Appeals for the District of Columbia Circuit.[173] At least one other challenge to the 8(a) Program is also pending in the federal district court for the District of Columbia,[174] and new challenges could potentially be filed in other jurisdictions, including the U.S. Court of Federal Claims.

Appeals from the Court of Federal Claims are heard by the U.S. Court of Appeals for the Federal Circuit, which, in its 2008 decision in *Rothe Development Corporation v. Department of Defense*, struck down a DOD contracting program that incorporated a similar presumption that minorities are disadvantaged.[175]

The *Rothe* court applied what is arguably a more stringent approach to equal protection analysis—and, particularly, the evidence compiled by Congress—than that applied by the *DynaLantic* court, and it is unclear how the 8(a) Program would fare if reviewed in light of *Rothe*.[176]

# Appendix. Comparison of the Requirements Pertaining to 8(a) Businesses Generally, Tribally Owned Businesses, ANC-Owned Businesses, and Others

| Requirements | 8(a) Businesses Generally | Tribally Owned 8(a) Businesses | ANC-Owned 8(a) Businesses | NHO-Owned 8(a) Businesses | CDC-Owned 8(a) Businesses |
|---|---|---|---|---|---|
| "Small" | Independentl y owned and operated; not dominant in field of operation; meets size standards (15 U.S.C. §631(a)) All affiliations count (13 C.F.R. §121.103) | Independently owned and operated; not dominant in field of operation; meets size standards (15 U.S.C. §631(a)) Affiliations based on the tribe or tribal ownership, among others, do not count (15 U.S.C. §636(j)(10)(J)(ii); 13 C.F.R. §124.109(c)(2)) | Independently owned and operated; not dominant in field of operation; meets size standards (15 U.S.C. §631(a)) Affiliations based on the ANC or ownership by the ANC, among others, do not count (15 U.S.C. §636(j)(10)(J)(ii); 13 C.F.R. §124.109(c)(2)) | Independently owned and operated; not dominant in field of operation; meets size standards (15 U.S.C. §631(a)) Affiliations based on the NHO or ownership by the NHO, among others, do not count (15 U.S.C. §636(j)(10)(J)(i); 13 C.F.R. §124.110(c)) | Independently owned and operated; not dominant in field of operation; meets size standards (15 U.S.C. §631(a)) Affiliations based on the CDC or ownership by the CDC, among others, do not count (15 U.S.C. §636(j)(10)(J)(ii); 13 C.F.R. §124.111(c)) |
| "Business" | For-profit entity with its place of business in the United States; operates primarily within the United States or makes a significant Contribution to the U.S. economy (13 C.F.R. §121.105(a)( 1)) | For-profit entity with its place of business in the United States; operates primarily within the United States or makes a Significant contribution to the U.S. economy (13 C.F.R. §121.105(a)(1)) | For-profit entity with its place of business in the United States; operates primarily within the United States or makes a significant contribution to the U.S. economy | For-profit entity with its place of business in the United States; operates primarily within the United Statesor makes a significant contribution to the U.S. economy (13 C.F.R. §121.105(a)(1)) | For-profit entity with its place of business in the United States; operates primarily within the United States or makes a significant contribution to the U.S. economy (13 C.F.R. §121.105(a)(1)) |

**(Continued)**

| Requirements | 8(a) Businesses Generally | Tribally Owned 8(a) Businesses | ANC-Owned 8(a) Businesses | NHO-Owned 8(a) Businesses | CDC-Owned 8(a) Businesses |
|---|---|---|---|---|---|
| | | | (13 C.F.R. §121.105(a)(1)) Although ANC may be non-profit, ANC-owned firms must be for-profit to be eligible for 8(a) Program (13 C.F.R. §124.109(a)(3)) | | |
| "Unconditionally owned and controlled" | At least 51% unconditional ly and directly owned by one or more disadvantage d individuals who are U.S. citizens (13 C.F.R. §124.105) Management and daily business operations must be conducted by one or more disadvantage d individuals (13 C.F.R.§124.106) | At least 51% tribally owned (13 C.F.R. §124.109(b)) Management may be conducted byindividuals who are not members of the tribe provided that the SBA determines that such management is necessary to assist the business's development, among other things (13 C.F.R.§124.109(c)(4)(B)) | At least 51% ANC-owned (13 C.F.R. §124.109(a)(3)) Management may be conducted by individuals who are not Alaska Natives provided that the SBA determines that such management is necessary to assist the business's development, among other things (13 C.F.R.§124.109(c)(4)(B)) | At least 51% NHO-owned (13 C.F.R. §124.110(a)) Not explicitly addressed inregulation[a] | At least 51% CDCowned (13 C.F.R. §124.111(a)) Management and daily business perations to be conducted by individuals having managerial experience of anextent and complexity needed torun the firm (13 C.F.R. 124.111(b)) |

| Requirements | 8(a) Businesses Generally | Tribally Owned 8(a) Businesses | ANC-Owned 8(a) Businesses | NHO-Owned 8(a) Businesses | CDC-Owned 8(a) Businesses |
|---|---|---|---|---|---|
| "Socially disadvantaged individual" | Members of designated groups presumed to be socially disadvantage d; other individuals may prove personal disadvantage by a preponderan ce of the evidence (13 C.F.R.§124.103) | Indian tribes presumed to be socially disadvantaged (43 U.S.C. §1626(e); 15 U.S.C. §637(a)(4)(A)-(B); 13 C.F.R. §124.109(b)(1)) | ANCs presumed to be socially disadvantaged (43 U.S.C. §1626(e); 15 U.S.C. §637(a)(4)(A)-(B); 13 C.F.R. §124.109(b)(1)) | NHOs presumed to be socially disadvantaged (43 U.S.C. §1626(e); 15 U.S.C. §637(a)(4)(A)-(B); 13 C.F.R. §124.109(b)(1)) | CDCs presumed to be socially disadvantaged (42 U.S.C. §9815(a)(2)) |
| "Economicallydi sadvantagedindi vidual" | Financial information (e.g., Personal income, personal net worth, fair market value of assets) must show diminished financial capital and credit opportunities (13 C.F.R. §124.104) | Tribe must prove economic disadvantage the first time a tribally owned firm applies to the 8(a) Program; thereafter, a tribe need only prove economic disadvantage at the request of the SBA (13 C.F.R. §124.109(b)(2)) | Deemed to be economically disadvantaged (43 U.S.C. §1626(e); 13 C.F.R.§124.109(a)(2)) | For first applicant to 8(a) Program, NHO members must meet the same initial eligibility economic disadvantage thresholds as individuallyowned 8(a) applicants; for later applicants, NHO members must meet the economic disadvantage thresholds for continued 8(a) eligibility (13 C.F.R. 24.110(c)(1) | CDCs presumed tobe economically disadvantaged (42U.S.C. §9815(a)(2)) |

**(Continued)**

| Require-ments | 8(a) Businesses Generally | Tribally Owned 8(a) Businesses | ANC-Owned 8(a) Businesses | NHO-Owned 8(a) Businesses | CDC-Owned 8(a) Businesses |
|---|---|---|---|---|---|
| "Good character" | No criminal conduct or violations of SBA regulations; cannot be debarred or suspended from government contracting (13 C.F.R. §124.108(a)) | No criminal conduct or violations of SBA regulations; cannot be debarred or suspended from government contracting (13 C.F.R. §124.108(a)) Requirement applies only toofficers, directors, and shareholders owning more than a 20% interest in the business, not to all members of the tribe (13 C.F.R.§124.109(c)(7)(B)(ii)) | No criminal conduct or violations of SBA regulations; cannot be debarred or suspended from government contracting (13 C.F.R. §124.108(a)) Requirement applies only to officers, directors, and shareholders owning more than a 20% interest in the business, not to all ANC shareholders (13 C.F.R. §124.109(c)(7)(B)(ii)) | No criminal conduct or violations of SBA regulations; cannot be debarred or suspended from government contracting (13 C.F.R. §124.108(a)) Regulations do not address to whom requirements apply[a] | No criminal conduct or violations of SBA regulations; cannot be debarred or suspended from government contracting (13 C.F.R. §124.108(a)) Requirements apply to the firm and "all its principals" (13 C.F.R. §124.111(g)) |

| Require-ments | 8(a) Businesses Generally | Tribally Owned 8(a) Businesses | ANC-Owned 8(a) Businesses | NHO-Owned 8(a) Businesses | CDC-Owned 8(a) Businesses |
|---|---|---|---|---|---|
| "Demonstra-ted potential for success" | Firm must generally have been in business in primary industry for at least two full years prior to date of application to 8(a) | Firm must have been in business in primary industry for at least two full years prior to date of application to 8(a) Program; | Firm must have been in business in primary industry for at least two full years prior to date of application to 8(a) Program; | Firm must have been in business in primary industry for at least two full years prior to date of application to 8(a) Program; | Firm must have been in business in primary industry for at least two full years prior to date of application to 8(a) Program; |
| | Program unless SBA grants a waiver; waiver based on 5 conditions[b] (13 C.F.R. §124.107) (13 C.F.R. §124.109(c)(6)(i)-(iii) | individuals whowill manage firm must have substantial experience, and firm must have had successful performance and adequate capital; or Tribe must have made written commitment to support the firm and have the financial ability to do so (13 C.F.R. §124.109(c)(6)(i)-(iii) | individuals who will manage firm must have substantial experience, and firm must have had successful performance and adequate capital; or ANC must have made written commitment to support the firm and have the financial ability to do so | individuals who will manage firm must have substantial experience, and firm must have had successful performance and adequate capital; or NHO must have madewritten commitment to support the firm and have the financial ability to do so (13 C.F.R. §124.110 (g)(1)-(3) | individuals who will manage firm must have substantial experience, and firm must have had successful performance and adequ te capital; or CDC must have made written commitment to support the firm and have the financial ability to do so(13 C.F.R. §124.111 (f)(1)-(3) |

**(Continued)**

| Requirements | 8(a) Businesses Generally | Tribally Owned 8(a) Businesses | ANC-Owned 8(a) Businesses | NHO-Owned 8(a) Businesses | CDC-Owned 8(a) Businesses |
|---|---|---|---|---|---|
| Sole-source awards | With contracts valued at over $4 million ($6.5 million for manufacturing g contracts), sole-source awards permissible only if there is not a reasonable expectation that at least two eligible 8(a) firms will submit offers and the award can be made at fair market price (48 C.F.R. §19.805-1(b)(1)-(2)) | Can be made with contracts valued at over $4 million ($6.5 million for manufacturing contracts) even if there is a reasonable expectation that at least two eligible 8(a) firms will submit offers and the award can be made at fair market price (15 U.S.C. §637(a)(1)(D)(i)-(ii); 48 C.F.R. §19.805-1(b)(1)-(2)) | Can be made with contracts valued at over $4 million ($6.5 million for manufacturing contracts) even if there is a reasonable expectation that at least two eligible 8(a) firms will submit offers and the award can be made at fair market price (15 U.S.C. §637(a)(1)(D)(i)-(ii); 48 C.F.R. §19.805-1(b)(1)-(2)) | Can be made with Department of Defense contracts valued at over $4 million ($6.5 million For manufacturing contracts) even if there is a reasonable Expectation that at least two eligible8(a) firms will submit offers and the award can be made at fair market price (48 C.F.R. §219.805-1(b)(2)(A)-(B)). | With contracts valued at over $4 million ($6.5 million for manufacturing)contracts, sole-source awards permissible only if there is not a reasonable expectation that at least two eligible 8(a) firms will submit offers and the award can be made at fair market price (48 C.F.R. §19.805-1(b)(1)-(2)) |

| Requirements | 8(a) Businesses Generally | Tribally Owned 8(a) Businesses | ANC-Owned 8(a) Businesses | NHO-Owned 8(a) Businesses | CDC-Owned 8(a) Businesses |
|---|---|---|---|---|---|
| | | | | Otherwise cannot be made unless there is not a reasonable expectation that at least two eligible 8(a) firms will submit offers and the award can be made at fair marketprice (48 C.F.R. §19.805-1(b)(1)-(2)) | |
| Inability to protest eligibility for award | Firm's eligibility for award cannot be challenged or protested as part of the solicitation or proposed contract award (48 C.F.R. §19.805-2(d)) | Firm's eligibility for award cannot be challenged or protested as part of the solicitation or proposed contract award (48 C.F.R. §19.805-2(d)) | Firm's eligibility for award cannot be challenged or protested as part of the solicitation or proposed contract award (48 C.F.R.§19.805-2(d)) | Firm's eligibility for award cannot be challenged or protested as part of the solicitation orproposed contract award (48 C.F.R. §19.805-2(d)) | Firm's eligibility for award cannot be challenged or protested as part of the solicitation or proposed contract award (48 C.F.R. §19.805-2(d)) |
| Maximum of nine years in the 8(a)Program | Firm receives "a program term of nine years" but could be terminated or graduated early (13 C.F.R.§124.2) | Firm receives "a program term of nine years" but could be terminated or graduated early (13 C.F.R. §124.2) | Firm receives "a program term of nine years" but could be terminated or graduated early (13 C.F.R. §124.2) | Firm receives "a program term of nine years" but could be terminated or graduated early (13 C.F.R. §124.2) | Firm receives "a program term of nine years" but could be terminated or graduated early (13 C.F.R. §124.2) |

**(Continued)**

| Requirements | 8(a) Businesses Generally | Tribally Owned 8(a) Businesses | ANC-Owned 8(a) Businesses | NHO-Owned 8(a) Businesses | CDC-Owned 8(a) Businesses |
|---|---|---|---|---|---|
| One-time eligibility for 8(a) Program | Applies to both disadvantage d owners and firms (13C.F.R. §124.108(b)) | Applies only to tribally owned firms, not tribes (15 U.S.C. §636(j)(11)(B)-(C)) | Applies only to ANC-owned firms, not ANCs (15 U.S.C. §636(j)(11)(B)-(C)) | Applies only to NHOowned firms, not NHOs (15 U.S.C. §636(j)(11)(B) -(C)) | Applies only to CDCowned firms, not CDCs (15 U.S.C. §636(j)(11)(B)-(C)) |
| Limits on the amount of 8(a) contracts that a firm may receive | No source awards possible once the firm has received combined total of competitive and solesource 8(a) contracts in excess of the dollar amount set forth in 13 C.F.R. §124.519 (13 C.F.R. §124.519(a)) Firms must receive an increasing percentage of revenue from non-8(a) sources throughout their participation in the 8(a) Program (13 C.F.R. §124.509(b)) | Can make solesource Awards even when a firm has received combined total of competitive and sole-source 8(a) contracts in excess of the dollar amount set forth in 13 C.F.R. §124.519 (13 C.F.R. §124.519(a)) Firms must receive an Increasing percentage of revenue from non-8(a) sources throughout their participation in the 8(a) Program (13 C.F.R.§124.509(b)) | Can make solesource awards even when a firm has combined total of competitive and sole-source 8(a) contracts in excess of the dollar amount set forth in 13 C.F.R. §124.519 (13 C.F.R. §124.519(a)) Firms must receive anIncreasing percentage of revenue from non-8(a) sources throughout their participation in the 8(a) Program (13 C.F.R. §124.509(b)) | Can make sole-source awards even when a firm has combined total of competitive and solesource 8 (a) contracts in excess of the dollar amount set forth in 13 C.F.R. §124.519 (13 C.F.R. §124.519(a)) Firms must receive an Increasing percentage of revenue from non-8(a) sources throughout their participation in the 8(a) Program (13 C.F.R. §124.509(b)) | Combined total of competitive and solesource 8(a) contracts in excess of the dollar amount set forth in 13 C.F.R. §124.519 not explicitly addressed in regulation Firms must receive an increasing percentage of revenue from non8( a) sources throughout their participation in the 8(a) Program (13 C.F.R. §124.509(b)) |

Source: Congressional Research Service.

[a] The rules governing NHO- and/or CDC-owned firms do not address this issue, and although the general rules apply where no "special rules" exist, it seems unlikely that NHO- and/or CDC-owned firms are treated differently than tribally or ANC-owned firms in this regard.

[b] These criteria include (1) the management experience of the disadvantaged individual(s) upon whom eligibility is based; (2) the business's technical experience; (3) the firm's capital; (4) the firm's performance record on prior federal or other contracts in its primary field of operations; and (5) whether the firm presently has, or can demonstrate its ability to timely obtain, the personnel, facilities, equipment, and other resources necessary to perform contracts under Section 8(a).

## End Notes

[1] See generally CRS Report R41945, Small Business Set-Aside Programs: An Overview and Recent Developments in the Law, by Kate M. Manuel and Erika K. Lunder. The 8(a) Program takes its name from one of the sections of the Small Business Act that authorizes it. The program is also governed by Section 7(j) of the act.

[2] See Small Business Goaling Report: Fiscal Year 2011, available at https://www.fpds.gov/downloads/top_requests/ FPDSNG_SB_Goaling_FY_2011.pdf. The report on FY2012 has not yet been compiled.

[3] Small Business Act of 1958, P.L. 85-536, §2(a), 72 Stat. 384 (July 18, 1958) (codified at 15 U.S.C. §631(a)).

[4] See, e.g., Phil Izzo, Recession Over in June 2009, Wall Street J., September 20, 2010, available at http://blogs.wsj.com/economics/2010/09/20/nber-recession-ended-in-june-2009/ (discus sing the recession of 2007- 2009).

[5] See, e.g., Small Bus. Admin., The Small Business Economy: A Report to the President 3 (2009), available at http://www.sba.gov/ADVO/research/sb_econ2009.pdf ("The credit freeze in the short-term funding market had a devastating effect on the economy and small firms."); John Rosenthal, Tough Times Often Even Tougher on Minority Biz, Chicago Business, November 30, 2009, available at http://www.chicagobusiness.com/cgibin/mag/article.pl? articleId=32738&seenIt=1.

[6] See, e.g., Mark Trumbull, Why Obama Job Creation Plan Focuses on Small Business, The Christian Science Monitor, December 8, 2009, available at http://features.csmonitor.com/politics/2009/12/08/why-obama-job-creation-planfocuses-on-small-business (noting that small businesses are reported to have created 65% of all new jobs in the United States over the past 15 years).

[7] Small Business Mobilization Act, P.L. 77-603, §4(f), 56 Stat. 351 (June 11, 1942).

[8] Act of July 31, 1951, P.L. 82-96, §110, 65 Stat. 131.

[9] P.L. 83-163, §207(c)-(d), 67 Stat. 230 (July 30, 1953).

[10] See, e.g., H.Rept. 494, 83rd Cong., 1st sess., at 2 (1953) (stating that the SBA would "continue many of the functions of the [SDPA] in the present mobilization period and in addition would be given powers and duties to encourage and assist small-business enterprises in peacetime as well as in any future war or mobilization period"); S.Rept. 1714, 85th Cong., 2nd sess., at 9-10 (1958) (stating that the act would "put[] the procurement assistance program on a peacetime basis").

[11] P.L. 85-536, §8(a)(1)-(2), 72 Stat. 384 (July 18, 1958).

[12] Id.

[13] Thomas Jefferson Hasty, III, Minority Business Enterprise Development and the Small Business Administration's8(a) Program: Past, Present, and (Is There a) Future? 145 Mil. L. Rev. 1, 8 (1994) ("[B]ecause the SBA believed that the efforts to start and operate an 8(a) program would not be worthwhile in terms of developing small business, the SBA's power to contract with other government agencies essentially went unused. The program actually lay dormant for about fifteen years until the racial atmosphere of the 1960s provided the impetus to wrestle the SBA's 8(a) authority from its dormant state.").

[14] Exec. Order No. 8802, 6 Federal Register 3,109 (June 25, 1941). Similar requirements were later imposed on nondefense contracts. See Exec. Order No. 9346, 8 Federal Register 7,182 (May 29, 1943).

[15] See, e.g., Exec. Order No. 10308, 16 Federal Register 12,303 (December 3, 1951) (Truman); Exec. Order No. 10557, 19 Federal Register 5,655 (September 3, 1954) (Eisenhower); Exec.

Order No. 10925, 26 Federal Register 1,977 (March 6, 1961) (Kennedy); Exec. Order No. 11458, 34 Federal Register 4,937 (March 7, 1969) (Nixon).

[16] Report of the National Advisory Commission on Civil Disorders 21 (1968).

[17] See, e.g., Hasty, supra note 13, at 11-12.

[18] See, e.g., Jonathan J. Bean, Big Government and Affirmative Action: The Scandalous History of the Small Business Administration 66 (2001).

[19] See Exec. Order No. 1625, 36 Federal Register 19,967 (October 13, 1971).

[20] 13 C.F.R. §124.8-1(b) (1970).

[21] 13 C.F.R. §124.8(c) (1973).

[22] S. Rep. No. 95-1070, 95th Cong., 2nd sess., at 14 (1978) ("One of the underlying reasons for the failure of this effort is that the program has no legislative basis."); H.Rept. 95-949, 95th Cong., 2nd sess., at 4 (1978) ("Congress has never extended legislative control over the activities of the 8(a) program, save through indirect appropriations, thereby permitting program operations.... [The] program is not as successful as it could be.").

[23] See, e.g., Ray Billie Trash Hauling, Inc. v. Kleppe, 477 F.2d 696, 703-04 (5th Cir. 1973). In this case, the court particularly noted that the SBA's program was supported by congressional and presidential mandates issued after enactment of the Small Business Act in 1958. Id. at 705.

[24] P.L. 95-507, 92 Stat. 1757 (October 24, 1978).

[25] Id. at §202.

[26] Id. (codified at 15 U.S.C. §637(a)(4)(A)-(B)). Firms that are owned and controlled by Indian tribes, ANCs, or NHOs were later included within the definition of a "socially and economically disadvantaged small business concern." See infra notes 36-43 and accompanying text.

[27] Id. (codified at 15 U.S.C. §637(a)(5)).

[28] Id. at §201 (codified at 15 U.S.C. §631(f)(1)(C)). The meaning of "socially disadvantaged individuals" was the subject of much debate at the time of the 1978 amendments. Some Members of Congress, perhaps focusing on the SBA's use of its authority under §8(a) in 1968-1970, viewed the 8(a) Program as a program for African Americans and would have defined "social disadvantage" accordingly. See, e.g., Parren J. Mitchell, Federal Affirmative Action for MBE's: An Historical Analysis, 1 Nat'l Bar Ass'n Mag. 46 (1983). Mitchell was a Member of the U.S. House of Representatives and leader of the Black Caucus when the 1978 amendments were enacted. Others favored a somewhat broader view, including both African Americans and Native Americans on the grounds that only those who did not come to the United States seeking the "American dream" should be deemed socially disadvantaged. See, e.g., Testimony Before the House Comm. on Small Bus., Subcomm. on General Oversight & Minority Enter., Task Force on Minority Enter., 96th Cong., at 21 (1979). Yet others suggested that groups that are not racial or ethnic minorities should be able to qualify as "socially disadvantaged," or that individuals ought to be able to prove they are personally socially disadvantaged even if they are not racial or ethnic minorities. See, e.g., H.Rept. 95-949, 95th Cong., 2nd sess., at 9 (1978) ("[T]he committee intends that the SBA give most serious consideration to, among others, women business owners" when determining which groups are socially disadvantaged.... [T]he bill does recognize that persons falling outside of the racial and ethnic groups presumed to be disadvantaged, may nevertheless be disadvantaged."). The bill that passed the House defined "socially disadvantaged individuals," in part, by establishing a rebuttable presumption that African Americans and Hispanic Americans are socially disadvantaged, while the bill that passed the Senate did not reference any racial or ethnic groups in defining "social disadvantage."

See, e.g., H.R. Conf. Rep. No. 95-1714, 95th Cong., 2nd sess., at 20 (1978); S.Rept. 95-1070, 95th Cong., 2nd sess., at 13-16 (1978). The conference committee reconciling the House and Senate versions ultimately arrived at a definition of "socially disadvantaged individuals" that was broader than the definition used in the SBA's 1973 regulation and included "those who have been subjected to racial or ethic prejudice or cultural bias because of their identity as a member of a group." P.L. 95-507, at §202. This definition did not incorporate the rebuttable presumption that members of certain groups are socially disadvantaged included in the House bill. However, the conference bill included congressional findings that "Black Americans, Hispanic Americans, Native Americans, and other minorities" are socially disadvantaged, thereby arguably achieving similar effect. Id. at §201.

[29] P.L. 95-507, at §202 (granting the SBA's Associate Administrator for Minority Small Business and Capital Ownership Development authority to make determinations regarding which other groups are socially disadvantaged); H.Rept. 95-949, supra note 28, at 9 (expressing the view that Sections 201 and 202 of the bill provide "sufficient discretion ... to allow SBA to designate any other additional minority group or persons it believes should be afforded the presumption of social ... disadvantage").

[30] See 13 C.F.R. §124.103(d)(2)(i)-(iii)(1980).

[31] 13 C.F.R. §124.103(b). Different groups are sometimes recognized as socially disadvantaged for purposes of other programs, such as those of the Department of Commerce's Minority Business Development Agency (MBDA). See 15 C.F.R. §1400.1(a). The SBA has rejected petitions from certain groups, including Hasidic Jews, women, disabled veterans, and Iranian-Americans. See, e.g., George R. La Noue & John C. Sullivan, Gross Presumptions: Determining Group Eligibility for Federal Procurement Preferences, 41 Santa Clara L. Rev. 103, 127-29 (2000). However, Hasidic Jews are eligible to receive assistance from the MBDA, while women are deemed to be disadvantaged for purposes of the Department of Transportation's Disadvantaged Business Enterprise (DBE) program. See 49 U.S.C. §47113(a)(2) (DBE program); 15 C.F.R. §1400.1(c) (MBDA program).

[32] 13 C.F.R. §124.103(c)(2) (standards of evidence for showing personal disadvantage); 13 C.F.R. §124.103(b)(3) (mechanisms for rebutting the presumption of social disadvantage).

[33] P.L. 95-507, §202.

[34] 13 C.F.R. §124.104(c)(2). Some commentators estimate that 80 to 90% of Americans are economically disadvantaged under the SBA's net-worth requirements. See, e.g., La Noue & Sullivan, supra note 31, at 108.

[35] 42 U.S.C. §9802.

[36] P.L. 97-35, Ch. 8, Subch. A, 95 Stat. 489 (1981) (codified at 42 U.S.C. §§9801 et seq.).

[37] Id. at §626, 95 Stat. 496 (codified at 42 U.S.C. §9815).

[38] P.L. 99-272, §18015, 100 Stat. 370 (1986) (codified at 15 U.S.C.§637(a)(13)) (defining "Indian tribe" to include "any Indian tribe, band, nation, or other organized group or community of Indians, including any Alaska Native village or regional or village corporation (within the meaning of the Alaska Native Claims Settlement Act (43 U.S.C.§1606)) which—(A) is recognized as eligible for the special programs and services provided by the United States to Indians because of their status as Indians, or (B) is recognized as such by the State in which such tribe, band, nation, group, or community resides."). An Alaska Native Corporation is "any Regional Corporation, Village Corporation, Urban Corporation or Group Corporation organized under laws of Alaska in accordance with the Alaska Native Claims Settlement Act." 13 C.F.R. §124.3. An Alaska Native is any "citizen of the United States who is a person of one-fourth degree or more

Alaskan Indian ..., Eskimo, Aleut blood, or a combination of those bloodlines. The term includes, in the absence of proof of a minimum blood quantum, any citizen whom a Native village or Native group regards as an Alaska Native if their father or mother is regarded as an Alaska Native." 13 C.F.R. §124.3.

[39] P.L. 99-272, §18015, 100 Stat. 370 (codified at 15 U.S.C. §637(a)(4)).

[40] P.L. 102-415, §10, 106 Stat. 2115 (1992) (codified at 43 U.S.C. §1626(e)).

[41] P.L. 100-656, §207, 102 Stat. 3861 (1988) (codified at 15 U.S.C. §637(a)(4)).

[42] Id. (codified at 15 U.S.C. §637(a)(15)). A "Native Hawaiian" is "any individual whose ancestors were natives, prior to 1778, of the area which now comprises the state of Hawaii." 13 C.F.R. §124.3.

[43] See, e.g., 13 C.F.R. §124.109(a) ("Special rules for ANCs. Small business concerns owned and controlled by ANCs are eligible for participation in the 8(a) program and must meet the eligibility criteria set forth in §124.112 to the extent the criteria are not inconsistent with this section.") (emphasis in original).

[44] See also CRS Report R40855, Contracting Programs for Alaska Native Corporations: Historical Development and Legal Authorities, by Kate M. Manuel, John R. Luckey, and Jane M. Smith (discussing contracting with ANC-owned firms through the 8(a) Program and other programs).

[45] 13 C.F.R. §124.101. The Office of Legal Counsel at the Department of Justice has opined that SBA regulations limiting eligibility for the 8(a) Program to citizens do not deprive resident aliens of due process in violation of the Fifth Amendment to the U.S. Constitution. See U.S. Dep't of Justice, Office of Legal Counsel, Constitutionality of 13 C.F.R. §124.103 Establishing Citizenship Requirement for Participation in 8(a) Program, March 4, 1996, available at http://www.justice.gov/olc/sba8.htm.

[46] The SBA's Office of Hearings and Appeals has, for example, developed a seven-part test for determining whether a small business is "unusually reliant" on a contractor that is used in determining affiliation. See Valenzuela Eng'g, Inc. & Curry Contracting Co., Inc., SBA-4151 (1996).

[47] See 13 C.F.R. §124.112 (a) ("In order for a concern ... to remain eligible for 8(a) ... program participation, it must continue to meet all eligibility criteria contained in [Section] 124.101 through [Section] 124.108.").

[48] 13 C.F.R. §121.105(a)(1). "Business" is separately defined for small agricultural cooperatives. See 13 C.F.R. §121.105(a)(2).

[49] 13 C.F.R. §121.105(b).

[50] 15 U.S.C. §632(a)(1)-(2)(A).

[51] 13 C.F.R. §§121.101-121.108. The number of employees is the average of each pay period for the preceding twelve calendar months. Gross income is based on the average for the last three completed fiscal years. It includes all revenues, not just those from the firm's primary industry. See IMDT, Inc., SBA-4121 (1995).

[52] 13 C.F.R. §121.201.

[53] 13 C.F.R. §121.103(a)(1). Control, or the power of control, need only exist. It need not be exercised for affiliation to be found.

[54] 13 C.F.R. §121.103(a)(6).

[55] 13 C.F.R. §121.103(h) ("[A] specific joint venture entity generally may not be awarded more than three contracts over a two year period, starting from the date of the award of the first contract, without the partners to the joint venture being deemed affiliated for all purposes.").

[56] 13 C.F.R. §121.103(h)(4) ("A contractor and its ostensible subcontractor are treated as joint venturers, and therefore affiliates, for size determination purposes. An ostensible

subcontractor is a subcontractor that performs primary and vital requirements of a contract, or of an order under a multiple award schedule contract, or a subcontractor upon which the prime contractor is unusually reliant.").

[57] 13 C.F.R. §121.103(i) ("Affiliation may arise ... through ... common ownership, common management or excessive restrictions on the sale of the franchise interest.").

[58] 15 U.S.C. §637(a)(4)(A)(i)-(ii) (requiring at least 51% unconditional ownership); 13 C.F.R. §124.105.

[59] 13 C.F.R. §124.3.

[60] 13 C.F.R. §124.105(a).

[61] 13 C.F.R. §124.105(h)(1). Ownership is limited to 10% when the 8(a) firm in is the "developmental stage" of the 8(a) Program and 20% when it is in the "transitional stage." Id. For more on the developmental and transitional stages, see infra notes 109-111 and accompanying text.

[62] 13 C.F.R. §124.105(h)(2).

[63] 15 U.S.C. §637(a)(4)(A)(i)-(ii) (requiring control of management and daily business operations); 13 C.F.R. §124.106.

[64] 13 C.F.R. §124.106.

[65] Id.

[66] 13 C.F.R. §124.106(a)(3).

[67] 13 C.F.R. §124.106(a)(2).

[68] 13 C.F.R. §124.106(e).

[69] 13 C.F.R. §124.106(e)(1) & (3).

[70] 13 C.F.R. §124.103(a). See also 15 U.S.C. §637(a)(5).

[71] 13 C.F.R. §124.103(b)(1). If required by the SBA, individuals claiming membership in these groups must demonstrate that they held themselves out and are recognized by others as members of the designated group(s). 13 C.F.R. §124.103(b)(2).

[72] 13 C.F.R. §124.103(b)(3).

[73] 13 C.F.R. §124.103(c)(1).

[74] 13 C.F.R. §124.103(c)(2)(i)-(iii).

[75] 13 C.F.R. §124.103(c)(2)(iii).

[76] 13 C.F.R. §124.103(d)(4). Groups petitioning for recognition as socially disadvantaged do not always obtain it. Over the years, the SBA has rejected petitions from Hasidic Jews, women, disabled veterans, and Iranian-Americans. See supra note 31.

[77] 13 C.F.R. §124.104(a). See also 15 U.S.C. §637(a)(6)(A).

[78] 13 C.F.R. §124.104(b)(1).

[79] 13 C.F.R. §124.104(c). See also 15 U.S.C. §637(a)(6)(E)(i)-(ii).

[80] 13 C.F.R. §124.104(c)(2).

[81] Id.

[82] Id.

[83] 13 C.F.R. §124.108(a)(1)-(5). For more on debarment and suspension, see CRS Report RL34753, Debarment and Suspension of Government Contractors: An Overview of the Law Including Recently Enacted and Proposed Amendments, by Kate M. Manuel.

[84] 13 C.F.R. §124.107. Specifically, "[i]ncome tax returns for each of the two previous tax years must show operating revenues in the primary industry in which the applicant is seeking 8(a) ... certification." 13 C.F.R. §124.107(a).

[85] 15 U.S.C. §637(a)(7)(A) ("reasonable prospects for success"); 13 C.F.R. §124.107(b)(1)(i)-(v).

[86] SBA may delegate the function of executing contracts to the procuring agencies and often does so. See 13 C.F.R. §124.501(a); Partnership Agreement Between the U.S. Small Business

Administration and the U.S. Department of Defense, September 27, 2012, available at http://www.acq.osd.mil/osbp/docs/dod-sba-8a-partnership-agreement20121031.pdf.

[87] Set-asides may be total or partial. See 48 C.F.R. §19.502-3(a).

[88] 15 U.S.C. §644(a) (describing when set-asides for small businesses are permissible); 41 U.S.C. §3303(b) (CICA provision authorizing set-asides for small businesses); 48 C.F.R. §§6.203-6.206 (set-asides for small business generally, 8(a) small businesses, Historically Underutilized Business Zone (HUBZone) small businesses, and service-disabled veteran-owned small businesses). CICA authorizes competitions excluding all sources other than small businesses when such competitions assure that a "fair proportion of the total purchases and contracts for property and services for the Federal Government shall be placed with small business concerns." 41 U.S.C. §3104. CICA also permits sole-source awards when such awards are made pursuant to a procedure expressly authorized by statute, or when special circumstances exist (e.g., urgent and compelling circumstances). See 10 U.S.C. §2304(c)(1) (defense agency procurements) & 41 U.S.C. §§3301 & 3304(a)(3)(A) (civilian agency procurements). For more on competition in federal contracting, see CRS Report R40516, Competition in Federal Contracting: An Overview of the Legal Requirements, by Kate M. Manuel.

[89] 15 U.S.C. §644(g)(1)-(2).

[90] They also count toward a separate goal for the percentage of federal procurement dollars awarded to small businesses generally. Currently, the government-wide goal is that 5% of all federal contract and subcontract dollars be spent with small disadvantaged businesses, including 8(a) businesses. Most agencies also have a 5% goal. See Small Business Goaling Report, supra note 7. The government-wide goal was met in FY2011, the most recent year for which information is available, when 7.67% of all federal procurement dollars was spent with small disadvantaged businesses. Id. Performance by the large procuring agencies varies, from 1.9% (Department of Energy) to 47.4% (SBA). Id.

[91] See 13 C.F.R. §124.1002 (defining "small disadvantaged business").

[92] See, e.g., AHNTECH, Inc., B-401092 (April 22, 2009) ("The [Small Business] Act affords the SBA and contracting agencies broad discretion in selecting procurements for the 8(a) program.").

[93] Even in this situation, SBA may accept the requirement under "extraordinary circumstances." 13 C.F.R. §124.504(a); Madison Servs., Inc., B-400615 (December 11, 2008) (finding that extraordinary circumstances existed when the agency's initial small business set-aside was erroneous and did not reflect its intentions).

[94] However, offers of requirements below the simplified acquisition threshold (generally $150,000) are "assume[d]" to have been accepted at the time they are made, and the agency may proceed with the award if it does not receive a reply from SBA within two days of sending the offer. 13 C.F.R. §124.503(a)(4)(i). See also Eagle Collaborative Computing Servs., Inc., B-401043.3 (January 28, 2011) (finding that an agency properly awarded a sole-source contract valued below the simplified acquisition threshold even though SBA never accepted the requirements).

[95] 13 C.F.R. §124.504(a)-(c). The third provision applies only to preexisting requirements. It does not apply to new contracts, follow-on or renewal contracts, or procurements under $150,000. Id. Also, under its regulations, SBA must presume an adverse impact when:

1) The small business concern has performed the specific requirement for at least 24 months;

2) The small business is performing the requirement at the time it is offered to the 8(a) ... program, or its performance of the requirement ended within 30 days of the procuring activity's offer of the requirement to the 8(a) ... program; and
3) The dollar value of the requirement that the small business is or was performing is 25 percent or more of its most recent annual gross sales (including those of its affiliates). 13 C.F.R. §124.504(c)(1)(i)(A)-(C).

[96] 15 U.S.C. §637(a)(1)(A); 48 C.F.R. §19.806(b). Fair market price is estimated by looking at recent prices for similar items or work, in the case of repeat purchases, or by considering commercial prices for similar products or services, available in-house cost estimates, cost or pricing data submitted by the contractor, or data from other government agencies, in the case of new purchases. 15 U.S.C. §637(a)(3)(B)(i)-(iii); 48 C.F.R. §19.807(b) & (c).

[97] 15 U.S.C. §637(a)(1)(A). See also Totolo v. United States, 87 Fed. Cl. 680, 695 (2009) ("The manner in which [an agency] assesses its needs is a business judgment and lies within its own discretionary domain."); JT Constr. Co., B254257 (December 6, 1993) (stating that it is a business judgment, within the contracting officer's discretion, to decide not to set aside a competition for small businesses). For a time in 2008-2010, the federal courts and the Government Accountability Office (GAO) found that set-asides for Historically Underutilized Business Zone (HUBZone) small businesses had "precedence" over set-asides for 8(a) firms. See generally CRS Report R40591, Set-Asides for Small Businesses: Recent Developments in the Law Regarding Precedence Among the Set-Aside Programs and Set-Asides Under Indefinite-Delivery/Indefinite-Quantity Contracts, by Kate M. Manuel. However, the Small Business Act was amended on September 27, 2010, to remove the language that formed the basis for these decisions. Small Business Jobs Act of 2010, P.L. 111-240, §1347,124 Stat. 2546-47 (September 27, 2010).

[98] See, e.g., Rothe Computer Solutions, LLC, B-299452 (May 9, 2007).

[99] 15 U.S.C. §637(a)(16)(A). A noncompetitive award may be made under this authority so long as (1) the firm is determined to be a responsible contractor for performance of the contract; (2) the award of the contract would be consistent with the firm's business plan; and (3) award of the contract would not result in the firm exceeding the percentage of revenue from 8(a) sources forecast in its annual business plan. 15 U.S.C. §637(a)(16)(A)(i)-(iii).

[100] 15 U.S.C. §637(a)(1)(D)(ii); 48 C.F.R. §19.805-1(d). However, competitive awards for contracts whose anticipated value is less than $4 million ($6.5 million for manufacturing contracts) can be made with the approval of the SBA's Associate Administrator for 8(a) Business Development. 15 U.S.C. §637(a)(1)(D)(i)(I)-(II); 48 C.F.R. §19.805-1(d).

[101] 48 C.F.R. §19.805-1(b)(1)-(2) (sole-source awards to tribally or ANC-owned firms); 48 C.F.R. §219.805- 1(b)(2)(A)-(B) (sole-source awards to NHO-owned firms). Prior to enactment of the National Defense Authorization Act (NDAA) for FY2010, contracting officers making sole-source awards in reliance on the second exception did not have to justify such awards or obtain approval of them from higher-level agency officials. The NDAA changed this by requiring justifications, approvals, and notices for sole-source contracts in excess of $20 million awarded under the authority of §8(a) similar to those required for sole-source contracts awarded under the general contracting authorities. Compare P.L. 111-84, §811, 123 Stat. 2405-06 (October 28, 2009) with 10 U.S.C. §2304(c) & (f) (procurements of defense agencies); 41 U.S.C. §3304(a) & (e) (procurements of civilian agencies).

[102] 48 C.F.R. §19.805-1(c).

[103] 48 C.F.R. §19.805-2(d).

[104] 15 U.S.C. §636(j)(10)(C)(i) (nine-year term); 15 U.S.C. §637(a)(9) (termination and early graduation); 13 C.F.R. §124.301 (exiting the 8(a) Program); 13 C.F.R. §124.302 (early graduation); 13 C.F.R. §124.303 (termination from the Program).

[105] 15 U.S.C. §636(j)(11)(B)-(C); 13 C.F.R. §124.108(b).

[106] 13 C.F.R. §124.108(b)(4).

[107] 13 C.F.R. §124.105(g)(1). SBA may waive this prohibition if the firms have no connections in terms of ownership, control, or contractual relationships. Id.

[108] 13 C.F.R. § 124.519(a)(1)-(2). Contracts less than $100,000 are not counted in determining whether a firm has reached the applicable limit. 13 C.F.R. § 124.519(a)(3). The Administrator of the SBA may waive this requirement if the head of the procuring agency determines that a sole-source award to a firm is necessary "to achieve significant interests of the Government." 13 C.F.R. § 124.519(e). Even after they have received a combined total of competitive and sole-source awards in excess of $100 million, or other applicable amount, firms may still receive competitive contracts under the 8(a) Program. 13 C.F.R. § 124.519(b).

[109] 15 U.S.C. §636(j)(10)(I)(i)-(iii); 13 C.F.R. §124.509(b)(1).

[110] 13 C.F.R. §124.509(b)(2).

[111] 13 C.F.R. §124.509(d)(1). This prohibition may be waived when the Director of the Office of Business Development finds that denial of a sole-source contract would cause severe economic hardship for the firm, potentially jeopardizing its survival, or when extenuating circumstances beyond the firm's control caused it to miss its target. 13 C.F.R. §125.509(e).

[112] 15 U.S.C. 637(a)(14)(A)-(B); 15 U.S.C. §644(o); 13 C.F.R. §125.6; 48 C.F.R. §52.219-14.

[113] 13 C.F.R. §124.510 (limits on subcontracting for 8(a) firms); 13 C.F.R. §125.6(a)(1)-(4) (limits on subcontracting for small businesses generally).

[114] 13 C.F.R. §124.109(c)(3)(i) (tribally and ANC-owned firms); 13 C.F.R. §124.110 (b) (NHO-owned firms); 13 C.F.R. §124.111(c) (CDC-owned firms).

[115] 13 C.F.R. §§124.109-124.111.

[116] 13 C.F.R. §124.109(c)(2)(i) (tribally and ANC-owned firms); 13 C.F.R. §124.110(b) (NHO-owned firms); 13 C.F.R. §124.111(c) (CDC-owned firms).

[117] 13 C.F.R. §124.109(c)(2)(iii) (tribally and ANC-owned firms); 13 C.F.R. §124.110(b) (NHO-owned firms); 13 C.F.R. §124.111(c) (CDC-owned firms). It is unclear how the language here, stating that "any other business enterprise owned by [an organization]" shall be excluded from the size determination, is to be reconciled with that in 13 C.F.R. §121.103(b)(2)(ii), which suggests that businesses owned and controlled by organizations could be found to be affiliates of the organization for reasons other than common ownership or management, or performance of common administrative services.

[118] See, e.g., Valenzuela Eng'g, Inc. & Curry Contracting Co., Inc., SBA-4151 (1996) (rejecting a challenge to the size of an ANC-owned firm because its subcontractor performed less than 25% of the work on the contract and was not its affiliate); Gov't Accountability Office, Increased Used of Alaska Native Corporations' Special 8(a) Provisions Calls for Tailored Oversight, GAO-06-399, at 29 (April 2006) (describing "early graduation" of ANC-owned 8(a) firms).

[119] 13 C.F.R. §124.109(a) & (b) (requiring tribally and ANC-owned firms to comply with the general eligibility requirements where they are not contrary to or inconsistent with the special requirements for these entities); 13 C.F.R. §124.110(a) (similar provision for NHO-owned firms); 13 C.F.R. §124.111(a) (similar provision for CDC-owned firms).

[120] 13 C.F.R. §124.109(a)(3).

[121] 13 C.F.R. §124.109(a) & (b) (requiring tribally and ANC-owned firms to comply with the general eligibility requirements where they are not contrary to or inconsistent with the special requirements for these entities); 13 C.F.R. §124.110(a) (similar provision for NHO-owned firms); 13 C.F.R. §124.111(a) (similar provision for CDC-owned firms).

[122] 13 C.F.R. §124.109(c)(4)(B).

[123] See 13 C.F.R. §124.110(d) (stating only that "[a]n individual responsible for the day-to-day management of an NHO-owned firm need not establish personal social and economic disadvantage").

[124] 13 C.F.R. §124.110(a) ("Concerns owned by economically disadvantaged Native Hawaiian Organizations, as defined in [Section] 124.3, are eligible for participation in the 8(a) program and other federal programs requiring SBA to determine social and economic disadvantage as a condition of eligibility. Such concerns must meet all eligibility criteria set forth in [Section] 124.101 through 124.108 and [Section] 124.112 to the extent that they are not inconsistent with this section.").

[125] 13 C.F.R. §124.111(b).

[126] 13 C.F.R. §124.109(b)(1) (tribally and ANC-owned firms); 15 U.S.C. §637(a)(4)(A)(i)(II) (NHO-owned firms); Small Disadvantaged Business Certification Application: Community Development Corporation (CDC) Owned Concern, OMB Approval No. 3245-0317 ("A Community Development Corporation (CDC) is considered to be a socially and economically disadvantaged entity if the parent CDC is a nonprofit organization responsible to residents of the area it serves which has received financial assistance under 42 U.S.C. 9805, et seq."). SBA's authority to designate CDCs as socially and economically disadvantaged derives from 42 U.S.C. §9815(a)(2). See 42 U.S.C. §9815(a)(2) ("Not later than 90 days after August 13, 1981, the Administrator of the Small Business Administration, after consultation with the Secretary, shall promulgate regulations to ensure the availability to community development corporations of such programs as shall further the purposes of this subchapter, including programs under §637(a) of title 15.").

[127] 43 U.S.C. §1626(e)(1) ("For all purposes of Federal law, a Native Corporation shall be considered to be a corporation owned and controlled by Natives and a minority and economically disadvantaged business enterprise if the Settlement Common Stock of the corporation and other stock of the corporation held by holders of Settlement Common Stock and by Natives and descendants of Natives, represents a majority of both the total equity of the corporation and the total voting power of the corporation for the purposes of electing directors."); 13 C.F.R. §124.109(a)(2) (same).

[128] See Small Disadvantaged Business Certification Application, supra note 125.

[129] 15 U.S.C. §637(a)(6)(A); 13 C.F.R. §124.109(b)(2)(i)-(vii).

[130] 13 C.F.R. §124.109(b).

[131] 13 C.F.R. §124.110(c)(1).

[132] Id. If the NHO has no members, then a majority of the members of the board of directors must qualify as economically disadvantaged.

[133] 13 C.F.R. §124.109(c)(7)(ii).

[134] See supra note 120 and accompanying text.

[135] 13 C.F.R. §124.111(g).

[136] 13 C.F.R. §124.109(c)(6)(i)-(iii) (ANC- and tribally-owned firms); 13 C.F.R. §124.110(g)(1)-(3) (NHO-owned firms); 13 C.F.R. §124.111(f)(1)-(3) (CDC-owned firms).

[137] See supra note 84 and accompanying text.

[138] See supra note 85 and accompanying text.

[139] Daniel K. Oakes, Inching Toward Balance: Reaching Proper Reform of the Alaska Native Corporations’ 8(a) Contracting Preferences, 40 Pub. Cont. L.J. 777 (2011).

[140] Regulations promulgated by SBA in February 2011 provided that this reporting requirement would be effective “as of September 9, 2011, unless SBA further delays implementation through a Notice in the Federal Register.” Small Bus. Admin., Small Business Size Regulations; 8(a) Business Development/Small Disadvantaged Business Status Determinations: Final Rule, 76 Federal Register 8222 (February 11, 2011). SBA appears to have delayed reporting through three such notices, two announcing tribal consultations about the reporting requirements, and a third announcing SBA’s intent to request approval of an information collection in accordance with the Paperwork Reduction Act of 1995. See Small Bus. Admin., 60 Day Notice and Request for Comments, 76 Federal Register 63983 (October 14, 2011); Small Bus. Admin., Notice of Tribal Consultations, 76 Federal Register 27859 (May 13, 2011); Small Bus. Admin., Notice of Tribal Consultations, 76 Federal Register 12273 (March 7, 2011).

[141] 13 C.F.R. §124.604.

[142] An Act To Amend the Small Business Act To Reform the Capital Ownership Development Program, and for Other Purposes; P.L. 100-656, §602(a), 102 Stat. 3887-88 (November 15, 1988) (codified at 15 U.S.C. §637 note); 48 C.F.R. §19.805-1(b)(2).

[143] The authority for DOD to make sole-source awards to NHO-owned firms of contracts valued at more than $4 million ($6.5 million for manufacturing contracts) even if contracting officers reasonably expect that offers will be received from at least two responsible small businesses existed on a temporary basis in 2004-2006 and became permanent in 2006. See Department of Defense, Emergency Supplemental Appropriations to Address Hurricanes in the Gulf of Mexico, and Pandemic Influenza Act of 2006, P.L. 109-148, §8020, 119 Stat. 2702-03 (December 30, 2005) (“[Provided] [t]hat, during the current fiscal year and hereafter, businesses certified as 8(a) by the Small Business Administration pursuant to section 8(a)(15) of Public Law 85-536, as amended, shall have the same status as other program participants under section 602 of P.L. 100-656 ... for purposes of contracting with agencies of the Department of Defense.”); 48 C.F.R. §219.805-1(b)(2)(A)-(B).

[144] See supra note 102.

[145] 13 C.F.R. §124.109(a) & (b) (requiring tribally and ANC-owned firms to comply with the general eligibility requirements where they are not contrary to or inconsistent with special requirements for these entities); 13 C.F.R. §124.110(a) (similar provision for NHO-owned firms); 13 C.F.R. §124.111(a) (similar provision for CDC-owned firms).

[146] 15 U.S.C. §644(o); 13 C.F.R. §125.6; 48 C.F.R. §52.219-14.

[147] 13 C.F.R. §124.109(a) & (b) (ANC- and tribally-owned firms); 13 C.F.R. §124.110(a) (NHO-owned firms); 13 C.F.R. §124.111(a) (CDC-owned firms).

[148] Id.; 15 U.S.C. §636(j)(11)(B)-(C).

[149] 13 C.F.R. §124.109(c)(3)(ii) (tribally and ANC-owned firms); 13 C.F.R. §124.110(e) (NHO-owned firms); 13 C.F.R. §124.111(d) (CDC-owned firms). These regulations also provide that an 8(a) firm owned by an ANC, Indian tribe, NHO, or CDC may not, within its first two years in the 8(a) Program, receive a sole-source contract that is a follow-on to an 8(a) contract currently performed by an 8(a) firm owned by that entity, or previously performed by an 8(a) firm owned by that entity that left the program within the past two years. Id. In addition, there are restrictions on the percentage of work that may be performed by any non-8(a) venturer(s) in joint ventures involving 8(a) firms. See generally 13 C.F.R. §124.513.

[150] 13 C.F.R. §124.109(c)(3)(ii) (tribally and ANC-owned firms); 13 C.F.R. §124.110(e) (NHO-owned firms); 13 C.F.R. §124.111(d) (CDC-owned firms).

[151] 13 C.F.R. §124.519(a). See supra note 108.

[152] 13 C.F.R. §124.509.

[153] See, e.g., Ray Baillie Trash Hauling, 477 F.3d at 710 ("The plaintiffs never applied for participation in the section 8(a) program. Furthermore, they do not even contend that they are socially or economically disadvantaged and therefore eligible for participation in the program."); SRS Techs., Inc. v. U.S. Dep't of Defense, No. 96-1484, 1997 U.S. App. LEXIS 10143 (4th Cir., May 6, 1997) ("SBA's requirement of economic disadvantage for entry into the 8(a) Program is a race-neutral criterion. It was by virtue of this race-neutral criterion that plaintiff failed to qualify for a contract award, and its standing to challenge the race-conscious criteria is therefore lacking."). But see C.S. McCrossan Constr. Co., Inc. v. Cook, No. 95-1345-HB, 1996 U.S. Dist. LEXIS 14721 (D.N.M., April 2, 1996) ("Although Defendants attempt to characterize this set-aside program as one based on size and economic status of the owner, the fact remains that 'economic disadvantage' requires a showing of 'social disadvantage' which then implicates the race-based challenge. ... Plaintiff is not seeking admission into the 8(a) program. It is challenging the government's preferential treatment towards 8(a) program participants in the bidding of the job order contract.").

[154] See, e.g., Cortez III Service Corp. v. Nat'l Aeronautics & Space Admin., 950 F. Supp. 357, 361 (D.D.C. 1996) (finding that the 8(a) Program is facially constitutional, but that "agencies have a responsibility to decide whether there has been a history of discrimination in the particular industry at issue" prior to procuring requirements through the 8(a) Program); Fordice Constr. Co. v. Marsh, 773 F. Supp. 867 (S.D. Miss. 1990) ("The court ... finds that the United States Army Corps of Engineers failed to give consideration to the impact of a 100% set-aside upon non-§8(a) eligible contractors in the Vicksburg area.").

[155] No. 95-2301 (EGS), 2012 U.S. Dist. LEXIS 114807 (D.D.C., August 15, 2012), at *29, *90. If the 8(a) Program as it presently exists, with its presumption that minorities are socially disadvantaged, were ever found to be unconstitutional on its face, the program could potentially be reconstituted without the presumption. Such a program might require proof of actual social disadvantage from all applicants to the 8(a) Program, perhaps using the same three criteria currently used by individual applicants demonstrating personal social disadvantage. See 13 C.F.R. §124.103(c)(2) (standards of evidence for showing personal disadvantage). Alternatively, the 8(a) Program could potentially continue as a program for small businesses owned by Indian tribes, ANCs, NHOs, or CDCs because tribes and other entities are generally not seen as constituting racial groups. Morton v. Mancari, 417 U.S. 535, 548 (1973) (treating the category of "Native Americans" as a political class, not a racial one, and describing programs targeting Native Americans as "reasonably designed to further the cause of Indian self-government"). The presumption of social and/or economic disadvantage accorded to these groups would thus not implicate a racial classification and would probably be subject only to "rational basis" review. Rational basis review is characterized by deference to legislative judgment, and the party challenging a government program must show that it is not rationally related to a legitimate government interest. See Craig v. Boren, 429 U.S. 190, 197 (1976).

[156] DynaLantic, 2012 U.S. Dist. LEXIS 114807, at *72.

[157] Id. at *31-*32. The court also rejected DynaLantic's argument that the government may only seek to remedy discrimination by a government entity, or by private individuals directly using government funds to discriminate. The court viewed these arguments as foreclosed by prior decisions holding that, under the Fourteenth Amendment, the government may implement race-conscious programs "to prevent itself from acting as a 'passive participant'

in private discrimination in the relevant industries or markets." Id. at 31 (quoting City of Richmond v. J.A. Croson, 488 U.S. 469, 492 (1989)).

[158] Id. at *40 ("Reports prepared by the GAO and investigations conducted by both the executive and legislative branches prior to the 1978 codification showed that the Section 8(a) program had fallen far short of its goal to develop businesses owned by disadvantaged individuals, and that one reason for this failure was that the program had no legislative basis.").

[159] Id. at *43 (quoting H.Rept. 1714, 95th Cong., 2nd sess., at 22-23 (1978)).

[160] Id. at *33-*34.

[161] Id. at *48. DynaLantic had asserted that post-enactment evidence of discrimination should not be considered. However, the court concluded that it was proper to consider such evidence, particularly where the "statute is over thirty years old and the evidence used to justify Section 8(a) [at the time of its enactment] is stale for purposes of determining a compelling interest in the present." Id.

[162] Id. at *132-*135.

[163] Id. at *137-*140.

[164] Id. at *144-*150.

[165] Adarand Constructors, Inc. v . Peña, 515 U.S. 200, 238 (1995).

[166] Grutter v. Bollinger, 539 U.S. 306, 341 (2003).

[167] DynaLantic, 2012 U.S. Dist. LEXIS 114807, at *120.

[168] Id. at *72. The government attempted to assert that, "as a matter of law, [it] need not tie evidence of discriminatory barriers to minority business formation and development to evidence of discrimination in any particular industry." Id. at *118. However, the court rejected this position as inconsistent with Supreme Court precedent, which it construed as making "clear that the government must provide evidence demonstrating there were eligible minorities in the relevant market ... that were denied entry or access notwithstanding their eligibility." Id.

[169] Id. at *154. DOD, however, has responded to the DynaLantic decision by prohibiting the award of contracts for "military simulators or any services in the military simulator industry," a prohibition that applies to "all future contract awards, including extensions of existing contracts or the exercise of options on existing contracts." Dep't of Defense, Office of the Under Secretary of Defense, Immediate Cessation of Small Business Development Program (8(a Program) Procurement Contracts for Military Simulators or Services in the Military Simulator Industry, August 22, 2012, available at http://www.acq.osd.mil/dpap/policy/policyvault/USA004988-12-DPAP.pdf. Some commentators have criticized this decision, in part, on the grounds that it prohibits the procurement of goods or services in this industry, while the DynaLantic decision addressed only goods. See, e.g., National Minority Organizations Respond to Federal DynaLantic Corp. Decision, PR Newswire, August 31, 2012, available at http://www.prnewswire.com/newsreleases/national-minority-organizations-respond-to-federal-court-dynalantic-corp-decision-168192866.html.

[170] See, e.g., Danielle Ivory, Minority Vendors Say Awards Program at Risk on U.S. Court Ruling, Bloomberg Gov't, September 13, 2012 (quoting Alan Chvotkin, counsel and executive vice president of the Professional Services Council, as saying that the DynaLantic ruling may "open the door to more lawsuits," and "[t]he implications across the government could be significant").

[171] See supra note 153 and accompanying text.

[172] See, e.g., Federal Spending Cuts Mean Fiercer Competition for Contractors and Higher Need for Market Research, According to US Federal Contractor Registration, SFGate, September

22, 2011, available at http://www.sfgate.com/ business/article/Federal-Spending-Cuts-Mean-Fiercer-Competition-2304840.php.

[173] See, e.g., Stewart Bishop, DynaLantic Appeals Ruling on Minority-Based Contracting, Law360, October 19, 2012, available at http://www.law360.com/articles/387961/ dynalantic-appeals-ruling-on-minority-based-contracting- (also noting the government's intent to appeal).

[174] Rothe Dev., Inc. v. Dep't of Defense, No. 12-CV-744, Original Complaint (filed D.D.C., May 9, 2012).

[175] 545 F.3d 1023 (Fed. Cir. 2008). For more on the Rothe decision, see generally CRS Report R40440, Rothe Development Corporation v. Department of Defense: The Constitutionality of Federal Contracting Programs for Minority-Owned and Other Small Businesses, by Jody Feder and Kate M. Manuel.

[176] In particular, the DynaLantic court relied on the precedent of United States v. Salerno in requiring that a plaintiff in a facial challenge must establish "that no set of circumstances exists under which [Section 8(a)] would be valid." DynaLantic, 2012 U.S. Dist. LEXIS 114807, at *23 (quoting Salerno, 481 U.S. 739, 745 (1987)). The Rothe court, in contrast, declined to apply this requirement of Salerno to the facial challenge to the program it struck down. See Rothe, 545 F.3d at 1032.

# INDEX

## C



## D

## E



## F



## G



## H

## N



## O



## P

## R



## S



## T

## U



## V



## W